Boyd Webb

Boyd Webb

The exhibition has been organised by the Whitechapel
Art Gallery and will be shown at the following venues:

Whitechapel Art Gallery, London (8 May – 21 June 1987)
Kestner-Gesellschaft, Hanover (17 July – 30 August 1987)
and thereafter at museums in the U.S.A.

Catalogue published by the Trustees of the Whitechapel Art Gallery, London
© The Author and the Trustees of the Whitechapel Art Gallery, 1987
Edited by Nicholas Serota and Joanna Skipwith
Designed by Richard Smith at Peter Saville Associates, London
Printed in Holland by Lecturis bv, Eindhoven
2000 copies printed and paperbound, May 1987
ISBN 0 85488 071 2

Contents

Lenders to the exhibition

Arrowhead Collection, Athens
Atlantis Museum, Tenerife
Jean Bernier Gallery, Athens
Karl Bornstein Gallery, Santa Monica
Collection of the Chase Manhattan Bank
Edwin C. Cohen, New York
Crousel-Hussenot Gallery, Paris
Anthony d'Offay Gallery, London
Wendy and Richard Hokin
Jeanne Meyers
Schlumberger Cambridge Research
Galerie Schurr, Stuttgart
Sonnabend Gallery, New York
Marlene Wossman
The artist
Private collections

Stedelijk Van Abbemuseum, Eindhoven
Leeds City Art Galleries
Arts Council of Great Britain, London
The Trustees of the Tate Gallery, London
The Trustees of the Victoria & Albert Museum, London
Fonds Régional d'Art Contemporain, Lyon
Fundacion Cultural Televisa, Mexico
Fonds National d'Art Contemporain, Paris
Musée National d'Art Moderne, Centre Georges Pompidou, Paris
City of Salford Art Galleries
Southampton City Art Gallery
Art Gallery of New South Wales, Sydney
Williams College Museum of Art, Williamstown, Massachussetts
Kunsthaus, Zürich

Foreword

They used to look like contemporary morality tales with just one clue missing, the inclusion of which might give logic and therefore purpose to the whole. Now Boyd Webb's work have assumed a more sombre mood. For the time being, at least, the actors have departed, and so have their props. The focus of attention has shifted from the absurdities of individual behaviour to a more poignant reflection on human and planetary existence.

Webb has always reminded us of the fragility of our personal worlds. The boundaries between real and imagined, between what we see, what we know and what we sense, are constantly redefining themselves. The simple and natural action of a child may look eccentric when repeated by an adult; 'normal' behaviour in one society may be regarded with apprehension or even disgust in another. We are all prisoners of convention, but the rules can change and we are then thrown into confusion or embarrassment.

'Rules' are important for Webb. They define our horizon and mark the rim of a flat earth. If we venture too far, we run the risk of falling into an abyss. Most of us remain firm 'flat earthers' tenaciously holding to the view that our own horizon is the limit. Webb's recent ventures, however, mark a move beyond this restriction, into planetary and terrestrial exploration on the one hand and microscopic investigation on the other. These works are a further testament of his ability to see the world afresh. He looks as if in turn through each end of the telescope, striking a fine balance between childlike wonderment and scientific observation. The structure of the world is thrown into doubt; simple perception it seems must be replaced by a complex reaction employing all our senses, including memory. We all know that the world is less logical than we choose to assume for peace of mind. Webb obliges us to suspend our order, deny ourselves the usual crutches and rely solely on the most tenuous faculty of all – innate comprehension.

This, the most comprehensive exhibition and publication of Webb's work to date, has been realised only through the close cooperation of the artist, his galleries on both sides of the Atlantic and the owners of his work, both private and institutional. We are most grateful for the friendly assistance which we have received from all concerned and, in particular, Jean Bernier in Athens and Robin Vousden of the Anthony d'Offay Gallery, London.

Nicholas Serota

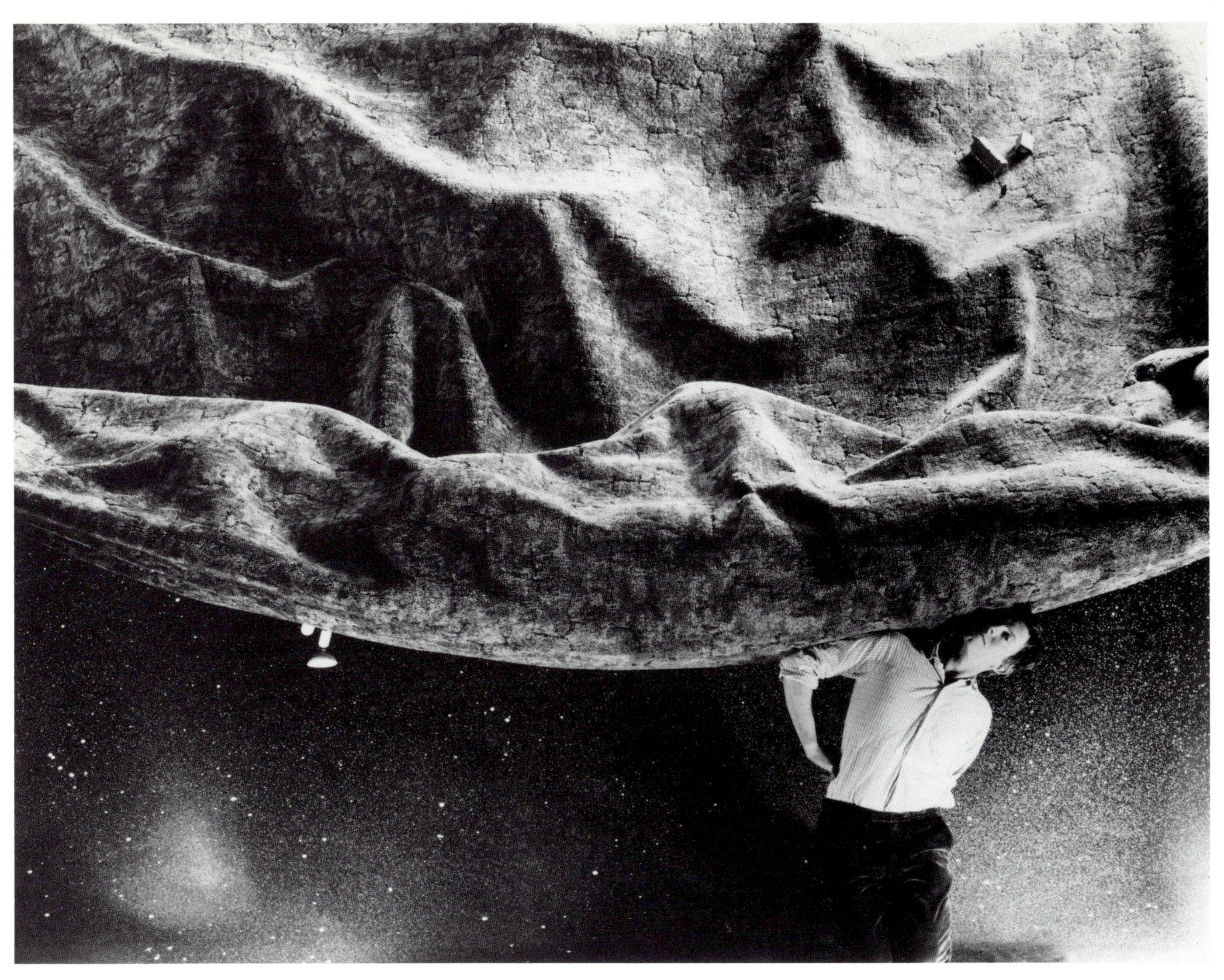

Eavesdroppist, 1984
123 × 154 cms
Unique colour photograph

Global Strategy

Stuart Morgan

Hanging in space, a naked god disports himself in true Olympian fashion. Grabbing one from an armful of spheres, he lobs it at a coconut on a shy on a neighbouring planet. And as it glides – slowly, weightlessly - he watches, consumed with interest at the grace of its trajectory, oblivious to anything but the path of the missile and the accuracy of his aim. His concentration parallels the attention the viewer pays him as part of a work of art to be rejected out of hand or accepted lock, stock and barrel. The soaring projectile is a model of a world. Our world at that. 'Like flies to wanton boys are we to the gods', says Gloucester in *King Lear*. 'They kill us for their sport'. But, before we criticise the deities for their indifference, we should remember the times we played football without a field, or goalposts, or even a proper ball. All we needed were rules, and even those could be bent a little.

If that replica of an earth provides a focus for the conceit of vastness, it also serves to dispel it. A second glance reveals that this particular globe, captured midway in its course, is no more than a child's toy of the kind that any high street shop might sell. Suddenly everything has changed. The god turns into a naked man, and the whole set-up looks fake; the heavens just rolls of spotted paper, the alien planet a piece of foam. One detail gives the game away: the pedestal on that flying sphere. But it does more; it shows that the whole episode really was play after all. One reaction would be to write off this detail as a mistake by the artist. But the title, **Trophy**, suggests that such a response would be wrong. Instead of concealing what could be a blemish, Webb is deliberately drawing attention to it.

But what is the 'trophy', exactly? Mounted on bases, globes resemble those awards for golf or ballroom dancing which deck the mantlepieces of champions. Eventually, of course, they cease to be proud of them. Demoted from such a prize-like status, this one is being thrown away to win an object scarcely worth winning: a coconut which, in a fairground, plays a double role, as an object to be knocked off its perch and the prize awarded to the lucky winner. One minute you throw things at it, the next you take it home. If we always set out to hit what we most wanted, we would still be cavemen, courting with clubs. Who wants to win a coconut anyway? Do we play to win ugly cups or medallions? Excusing his throwing the globe was one thing. But if he is only going to win a large nut that he may not really want, perhaps we should revise our lenient view of the game he is playing and the game we are deciding to play as we watch. Maybe it does matter whether the globe is a toy, or real, after all. Perhaps Boyd Webb, who made **Trophy**, is playing his own game too - a double game. Flaunting the power of fiction, he simultaneously lays it bare. His work is a fabrication, in the fullest sense of the word.

No name exists for the genre Webb has perfected. Though the product is a cibachrome photograph, 'photography' in most senses of the word cannot accommodate the fact that he constructs what he then records. He is more than a sculptor who simply documents his work. Without the framing, the flattening, the sheer 'otherness' of the world seen through a viewfinder, his art could be written off as eccentricity, the hobby of an oddball with a perverse attitude to materials. In fact, his basic gesture – the making, photographing and destruction of flimsy, purpose-built sets – constitutes a critique of both photography and sculpture at the same time. And if, as in **Trophy**, an entire reading hangs on a single detail, the issue of genre depends on the same detail, looked at in another way. Why is it a globe that can be bought in a shop and not, as it might be in a stage design, a prop made from scratch? Some dual scepticism is implied, not only of these media in themselves, but of preconceptions which have governed their practice: documentation on the one hand and literalism on the other, the assumption that a sculpture necessarily partakes of, or reveals, some essence of its material. Both imply a certain moral stance as well as a confusion of means and ends. But if such proprieties were always observed, some art forms might never exist at all. Can opera be justified by anything other than its effect? Operatic though it is, Webb's position is studied rather than natural, formulated during a period when both sculptural and photographic premises were being re-examined, and their relationship to each other was under discussion.

By the end of the 1960s the challenge to sculpture in its traditional manifestations had never been greater. Elitism and commodity fetishism, the trappings of a late capitalist society, had diverted art from its true aims, the argument ran. Not even the ideals of Russian Constructivism had prevented a postwar swerve back to nineteenth-century assumptions. Earth art, body art, performance and other developments arose from a need to multiply the means by which the 'object' of art could be re-assessed. Art could be a phrase, or a gesture, or a change in the environment. It could be a philosophical disquisition, or a batch of postcards, or meeting a stranger …

Possibilities proliferated, not in a destructive spirit, but as part of a fullscale attempt to restore the revolutionary potential of art as early Modernists had understood it. The attempt was international, as major art movements in the first thirty years of the twentieth century had been, and it was disseminated by art magazines, which is to say, by a combination of criticism and photography. Suddenly their function was hotly debated. To what extent was criticism itself a creative act? And what of photography? Did it provide an accurate report of art works? Was the photographer inevitably interpreting what he saw and making an art work of his or her own? Predictably, the burden placed on photography at this time, as documentation of art too distant, or temporary, or private to be experienced in any other way, resulted in art made specifically for the camera. But it also led to an examination of the kind of information a photograph communicated. Bertolt Brecht once pointed out that a photographic image which lacks a text is both incomplete and morally questionable, since although it may show, for example, one army attacking another, it fails to indicate which is in the right. The medium's dependence on context as a major regulator of meaning pushed it to the forefront of discussion in this turn-of-the-decade investigation. New genres emerged, like the 'phototext sequence' or 'story art', in which verbal and visual components existed in a state of mutual critique. New artists emerged too, like Boyd Webb.

As a sculpture student in Christchurch, New Zealand, Webb had been exposed to the same influences as any other artist anywhere else in the world. Only the distance from major centres of activity may have made a difference. Could this be the reason why major New Zealand artists sometimes have the air of inventors, redefining their media to suit themselves? Late in seeing Cubism, Colin McCahon devoted his early years to looking at prices written on the blackboards of roadside fruit stalls and noticing the way figures and letters were grouped on cricket scoreboards before eventually arriving at his own mixture of symbol and

calligraphy. As a young and naughty child, Len Lye was thrown out of the house one day and found himself in a sunny orchard he knew well. Sheer petulance made him kick the nearest object he could see, a shiny petrol can, and, astonished at the simultaneous flash, noise and impact, he sat down and thought about it, his anger forgotten completely. Years later he conceived his own art form, a mixture of light, movement and sound, using reflecting metal. No comparable story exists about Boyd Webb, whose first art school projects set out to contradict the expectations of the staff. Collections of debris placed outdoors made it look as if the sea had washed it up that far, while a short film, shot frame by frame, showed an underground tennis match with the tips of the racquets sticking out of the lawn and the umpire, visible only from the waist up, following the ball with his eyes. Webb's Christchurch masterpiece was his degree show. A notice on a locked door showed the hours when he would be available. Examiners returned between the stated hours only to find a small office with a secretary who told them politely that Mr Webb was busy and that they needed to make an appointment.
 When they were finally admitted to the inner office they found evidence of his work in alphabetical order in a filing cabinet.

The entire exercise resembles what happens when quotation marks are placed around a sentence; in terms of events, everyday life has suddenly assumed a theatrical air, as if held aloft like a specimen on tweezers. Could this defamiliarisation be transferred to art? In 1970

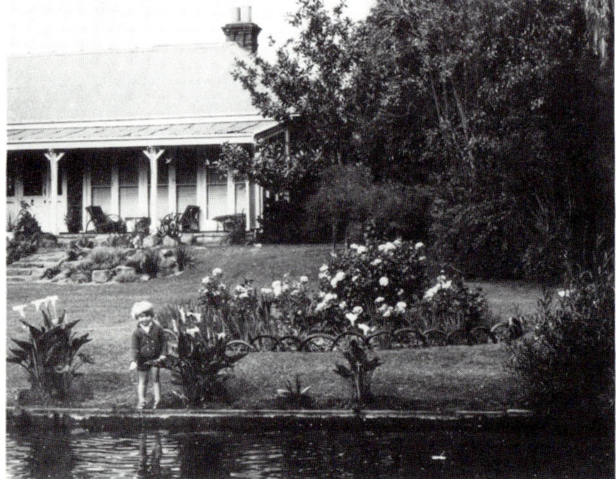

1. **Eels,** 1971
Black and white photograph
29.5 X 37.5 cms

he made a work which showed that it could (fig. 1). The scene is pure family-album fodder. Wreathed in smiles, an angelic child stands in the front garden of a bungalow. The sun is shining, flowers are blooming, all's right with the world. Except, perhaps, one tiny detail. Surrounding a circular flower-bed is a low fence made of loops of metal stuck into the ground. A closer look reveals that they are not metal, certainly not painted, and far too thick to be plausible. In fact, the fence is made of frozen eels, bent into semicircles, thawing quickly in the heat. In quite a different way from the usual perception of snapshots, the photograph has been offered as a kind of forgery. And the principle of the disturbing detail comes into play for the first time, indicating the presence of an artist where it is least expected. As in the case of the subterranean tennis, worlds collide in classic Surrealist fashion. More interesting is the fact that the interpolated object demands to be read as evidence which calls the context of the photograph into question. This sense of rupture or displacement was to become Webb's stock-in-trade. Interpretable as an error, part of what he calls his 'usual tacky style', the detail is like a passer-by who walks through the wrong door and finds he has been mistaken for the groom at a wedding. He may act as an adequate stand-in. He may even decide to go through with the ceremony. He and his wife may have three children and live happily ever after. But the sense that he is a foreign element who has been subsumed, but never fully accommodated, will never leave him. Nor, perhaps, will the sense that something funny happened. Removal of context, humour and photographic subversion feature equally in the works Webb made in the sculpture school at the Royal College of Art, meetings of words and images in which a lurking portentousness was undermined by the improvised quality of the entire enterprise.

Webb has always avoided working with professional models. Instead, he chooses his cast according to physique and demeanour to suit the formal qualities a particular photograph demands. In addition, he insists on a certain blankness, a high forgettability quotient, in order to circumvent the entire question of role-playing. In these early works locales were also plausible but unmemorable. Bewildered by the size and variety of London, Webb spent his time cycling about, noting likely locations for what, incidentally, became a series of vignettes of British characters and customs. Major works of art have been made about countries unknown to their creators; in *The Secret Agent,* for

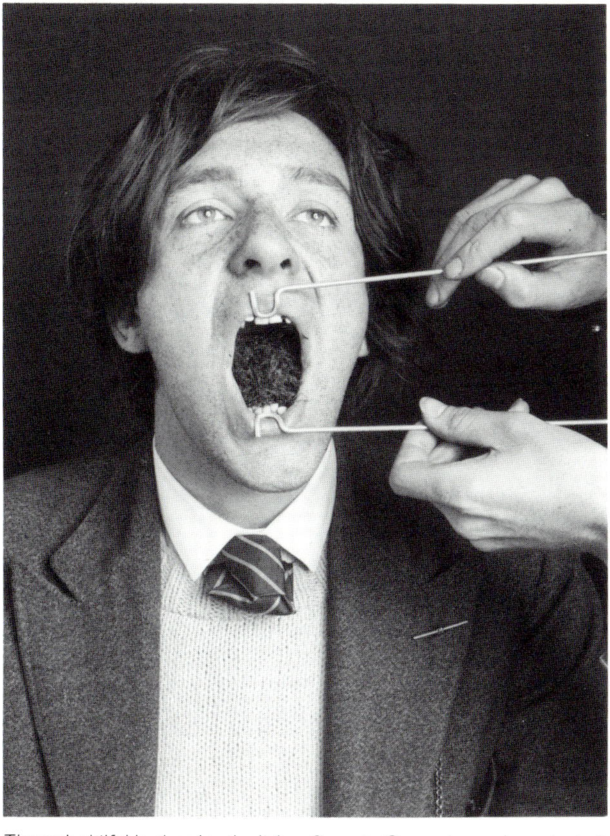

Herbert Groves, an amateur lichenologist, has successfully developed
and introduced a lichen (Sponsio Grovesiaceae) to the moist lining of
his throat in order to become eligible for disability compensation.
A keen punter he now studies form in earnest, investing sometimes to
advantage, sometimes not.

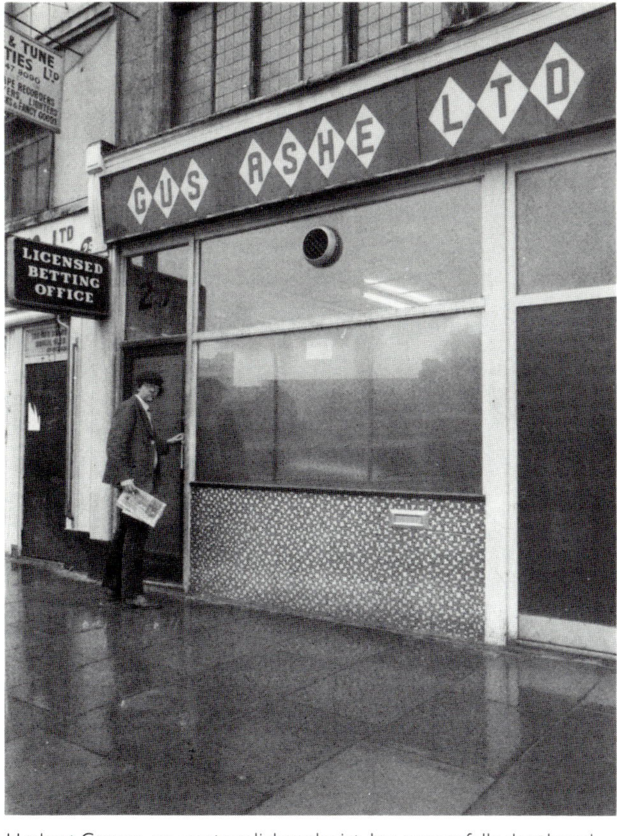

Through skilful husbandry the lichen Sponsio Grovesiaceae has adapted
successfully to the inclement environment of the human throat.
Nutrients essential for this lichen's survival are filtered from the humid
fug of despair, jubilation and nervous human effluvium peculiar to
betting shops.

2. **Herbert Groves,** 1973
    Colour photographs
    21 × 15 cms each

example, Joseph Conrad amalgamated what he knew of
London from reading Charles Dickens and H.G. Wells.
Webb's England, refracted as it is through the eyes of
someone from another hemisphere, turns out to be a
country bristling with eccentrics and tricksters, run
according to rules laid down only to be broken again.
Lubricated by bribery, punctuated by trivial slights, life in
the metropolis smacks of postwar austerity. Even
Webb's later choice of appliances recall the same period:
telephones, toasters, suitcases, furniture, linoleum, and
the thick glasses in which milkshakes are served. This is
not a cosy place. Alongside settled domestic types are
vagrants gambling in empty lots, a woman who drops her
baby while concerned with her own problems, a poacher

with the same unreliable characteristics as his dog, all
reminders that life is neither easy nor smug in a capital
city which loses all resemblance to modern London and
comes to resemble a closed fictional realm, devised for
the convenience of the artist himself.

In each work from this period the structure
differs and the plots vary in length. Webb was working
hard to discover ways of combining his chosen elements.
In **Herbert Groves** (fig. 2), for instance, the two parts of
the work are linked by the idea of symbiosis. Lichen,
which Groves cultivates in his mouth, consists of fungus
and algae living off each other. So Groves must frequent
betting shops in order to be able to malinger, and he
himself exists as the link between gambling, which is

cyclical and compulsive, and lichenology, the study of a
repeated closed circuit. Despite this, the entire plot has
the air of a device, designed to bring together two
unlikely photographs, one informal and non-specific in
tone, and the other, a man with a mouth full of moss held
open in mock-medical manner with what look more like
skewers than surgical implements, obviously made to
prove a point. Could the story be an excuse to link
unrelated elements? After all, Raymond Roussel wrote
that way.

Considering the near-impossibility of finding
solutions to the problem of linking words and images in
ways which matched verbal with visual devices, it is
hardly surprising that the recognisable Boyd Webb
format took so long to perfect. That it finally seems to
solve itself is no surprise as eventually the problem
almost became the theme of the works. From this grew
the prevalence of arguments as plots, and a concern with
impossible grafts, combinations and marriages. The
breakthrough came with one such piece. An early story
of a woman determined to revenge herself symbolically
on her domineering spouse by persuading him to
armwrestle her over the breakfast table, then cheating
and forcing his clean shirtcuff down into a cornflake bowl
full of mud, had demanded a lengthy text, a picture of the
competition itself and a flashback to her, wading in the
river to gather mud. Whereas **Worms** (fig. 3), the
prototype of the mature style, carried only a one-word
title and showed two men holding a tug-of-war in a
closed room.

In this instance the photograph itself
commands the viewer's attention. The protagonists are
so evenly matched that the handkerchief marking the
middle of the rope occurs exactly at the mid-point of the
photograph. Inset above them, like a picture on al wall, is

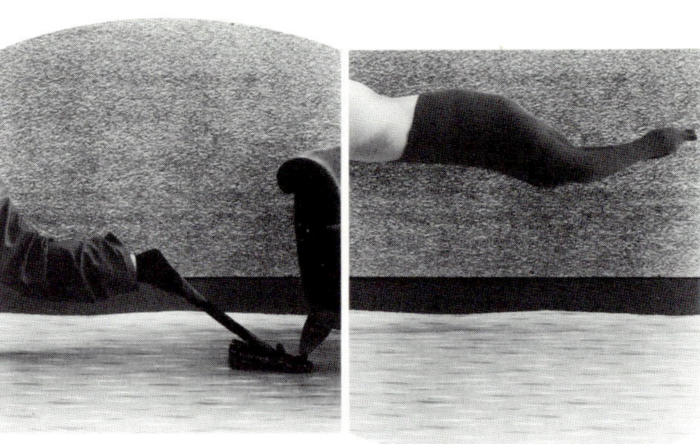

3. **Worms,** 1977
Colour photograph
17.5 × 31 cms

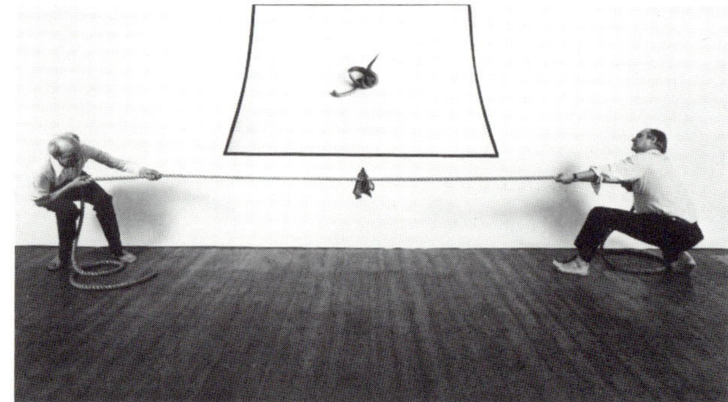

4. **Distressed Hose,** 1980
Colour photographs
28 × 23 cms each

an image of two worms, knotted together like a pair of
bent nails. Tweedledum and Tweedledee agreed to fight
every day on very little pretext. In the same way, these
figures seem locked in a combat which transcends
immediate issues. Their motionlessness; the opposition
between the singularity and tautness of the rope and
complexity and looseness of the tangled worms; the
expectation inherited from the Middle Ages that combat
demands an heraldic emblem, all hint at a tussle of
unusual significance. Yet even this cannot detract from
the silliness of it all. Two men in a room, indeed, and a
couple of garden worms. From this point on, all that was
needed was to integrate titles and images more fully
until, by the 1980s, titles would exist as poems in their
own right, feeding off photographs which nourish them in
return. Boyd Webb titles like **Biltong, Sphagnum,
Torque, Enzyme,** resemble crossword-puzzle solutions
arrived at only after excruciating mental gymnastics.
Finally, correctly, Webb decided that these were the
only context his work required.

The first stage was to trim his texts to the
bone; the presentation of images remained a problem.
Realising that photographs seldom command the same
degree of attention as paintings, Webb set out to
heighten their status as objects in their own right. Some
were shaped, a ploy which worked perfectly only when
the images were at their most abstract, as in **Distressed
Hose** (fig. 4). Others were mounted so that they could
hang free of the back of the frame or bulge gently at the
sides. A similar problem existed with regard to texts.
Whereas longer passages needed to be separated from
the image itself, later solutions included writing the
words in ink along the bottom of the picture or,

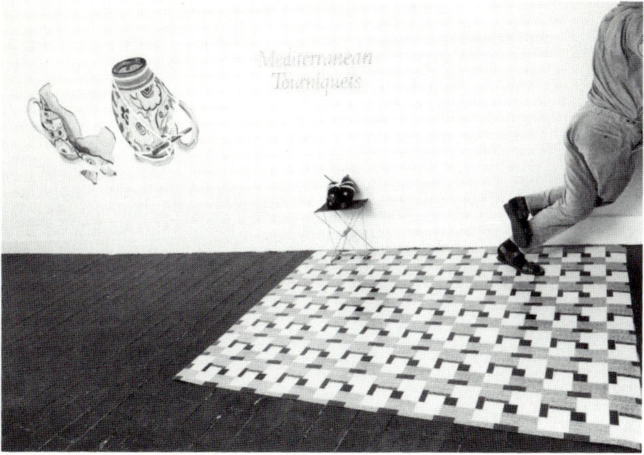

5. **Mediterranean Tourniquets**, 1979
Colour photograph
27 × 37 cms

unusually, making them part of the ensemble.
Mediterranean Tourniquets (fig. 5) is an example of this and other routes he decided not to follow. Writing, a drawing of an object, a 'sculpture' made of aubergines and what could loosely be described as dance all meet in this episodic piece, the humour of which derives from its subtext: the British summer holiday. Those sandals and the folding stool speak volumes. Rather than being dealt with separately, ruins, accidents, shopping for exotic vegetables and the inevitable stomach upset are drawn loosely together into a single unit. The structure ends as a kind of picaresque; it begins and ends but everything in between is allowed equal weight, and there is no particular reason why the left to right panorama should not continue indefinitely. Such a structure reduced the impact of its individual parts. Furthermore giving such prominence to the title was not always desirable. When titles were written on the photographs there was a danger of confusing the work with the autobiographical use of handwriting sanctioned by feminists, in particular, but borrowed by male photographers such as Duane Michals. Such a confessional tone was irrelevant to Webb's needs. But this and other problems were not fully solved until 1982, when he began to make cibachromes, so large in relation to the writing that text ceased to play a prominent visual role.

Though the reasons for this final innovation can all be located within the evolution of Webb's work itself, one parallel development, not an influence but a force too large to be ignored during his formative years, was a form of advertising more advanced in Britain than

anywhere else in the world. Such advertisements lean heavily on conventions of British conversation like understatement and obliquity as well as peculiarities such as Spoonerisms, shaggy dog stories and running jokes. Above all, they have been marked by their insouciant approach to selling, quite different in tone from that of their North American counterparts. After being warned of the mediocrity of British cinema, Federico Fellini once visited Britain and left raving about the 'masterpieces' shown before and between the featured films. Gradual improvement in quality has been accompanied by an increase in subtlety; campaigns have even been be launched which never mention the name of the product but which allude to the campaigns of competitors.

For Webb the increased awareness that this demands must have created a more perceptive audience for his work. Furthermore, advertising offers an aesthetic parallel to his own. Yet observing its growth may only have strengthened his resolve. In Britain advertising commandeered conceptual art, stole its techniques, nullified its political stance and left it helpless. Corporate identity symbols, the growing subliminality of, say, cigarette advertising, the full-scale selling of entire political parties by up-to-date methods, made conceptual art and its aims seem puny and countrified. Without a single assistant, without expensive equipment, without a budget of millions, Webb continued working behind locked doors.

From behind those doors the question of interface between visual and verbal proved to be the cutting edge of the entire project. Different languages remain different languages, as demonstrated by the wordbound scholar in **Cipher and Decipher**, unable to puzzle out what signal is being given by a ballet-dancer with a broken arm. And different elements remain different elements, as **Mediterranean Tourniquets** seems to acknowledge, with its repeated motif of parts forced uncomfortably together. Webb was determined that the way of working he developed would be neither transparent nor pure. For him, opacity, the need to make people point and ask 'What is it?' at the same time as 'What does it mean?', even to the point of being led on wild goose-chases, went hand in hand with…. illegitimacy? Sadly, the term exists only as a negative, with overtones of purity soiled. After reading Robert Smithson's account of driving at night through the New Jersey Turnpike, an experience he compared favourably with every work of art he had ever seen, critic Michael Fried wrote his classic essay 'Art and Objecthood', sealing the fate of one entire approach to art and furnishing opponents – Minimal, Post-Minimal and conceptual artists of the time – with arguments to rebuff for several years thereafter.

Never intended as art, the Turnpike might produce pleasing incidental effects, Fried felt, but it lacked sculpture's concentration, deliberacy, its tested sense of form and colour and its function as part of an ongoing debate. Sculpture, he concluded, was a language which demanded discussion in its own terms. Fried was fighting a losing battle. But the way he fought was the reason he lost. Henceforth, visual art would be concerned with precisely the area he regarded as incoherent collage. And since Fried seemed to be defining reality as much as art, when his opponents had disposed of the premise that art occupies only a single plane of reality, the way was open for a new cross-breed. 'Theatre', Fried called it, disapprovingly, though the choice of term may have been misguided. Boyd Webb's deliberate illegitimacy involved creating a mixed response in the viewer, half in and half out of a reaction to art as a known quantity. His particular 'theatre' is one where Hamlet spots his mother-in-law sitting in the second row, walks to the front of the stage and chats to her for a while before returning to the battlements at Elsinore. Photography was the obvious choice of medium for an artist intent on opting for two simultaneous definitions of reality and on bouncing back and forth between them; looking at photographs is a matter of looking into as well as at, of considering what is depicted as well as the way it is depicted. It is easy to understand Webb's constant desire to maintain a consciousness of the photograph as object, to delay the act of looking through it, as well as his urge to exaggerate the extremes between which he oscillates: to make his work as stagey as possible on the one hand and on the other to disorientate the viewer by offering impossible details like frozen eels. Only in retrospect is it possible to spot some rhetoric at work in this ricochet reaction. Halfway between the definitions of reality proposed by Sophocles and the fence of eels lies the one he most wants to emphasise: the everyday. It was only a matter of time before he began to examine the assumptions behind his own techniques which stressed this factor.

In *Tableaux*, a selection of his work published in 1978, Webb acknowledged his affinity with the nineteenth-century. 'A series of lame but colourful cartoons', he called it, 'combining the concerns of the Victorian genre painter and the technique of the mail-order catalogue photographer'. Implicit in this private

ancestry is the approach which most distinguishes Webb's work from that of other proponents of what is sometimes called 'staged photography'. In mail order catalogues objects are recorded. Nothing more. In Victorian genre painting, as in Victorian culture generally, good triumphs over evil. But why connect the two? The refusal to retouch, or make alterations of scale, sets Webb's work apart from one entire school of British photographic trickery, like that of Angus McBean for example. After actors have been posed and sets arranged, the picture is taken with a plate camera – Webb sees the image upside down – then the film is developed. Nothing more. And the morality of such a 'straight' approach, the mere act of recording a sculptural set-piece, filters through to the 'morality' of producing such a thing in the first place, without continuing to make an entire sculpture. Yet, once more, Webb's honesty counters the demand for permanence. Far from claiming that they are permanent, he exposes his own artifice at every turn.

It is obvious that however closely they resemble their more permanent counterparts, props which are not made to last cannot offer one-to-one representations. In Webb's work the use of actual objects only produces a greater richness of analogy. In **Lung**, for instance, the boat from which a rescuer drops his lifeline resembles not a boat but a bathtub, a change which means that the viewer is made aware that his physical position is far more precarious than he realises. Yet the lip of the tub combined with another cue, the black roll-neck sweater, suggest that this could be a pulpit and the man a preacher. Baths are miniature seas where children, and not only children, sail their boats. In his bath, which is also a boat, the water is outside, not in. The man must feel like a fish out of water, but that may soon be rectified. In his bath, which is also a pulpit, he will work no miracles, unlike Jesus who walked upon the water at Galilee. Indeed, he seems incapable of carrying out a simple act of first aid. So the associations of such a reading proliferate. That the bathtub is not a real bathtub, but might well be, opens up another argument entirely – against identifying isolated pockets of meaning and regarding them as indicators of dramatic irony. One could argue that Webb is an abstractionist searching for an entire visual language which should be construed as a totality, not item by item. Simply looking endorses this reaction; **Samurai** or **Glorious Morning** are greater decorative works than any living British painter could match. Yet as an argument the idea of Webb as an abstractionist is just too easy; so much of his art depends on a kind of failure, a visible, even wilful, refusal to take sanctioned decisions. The perversity of combing and trimming steel wool until it resembles an eighteenth-century wig in **Coda**, painting the tip of an Indian vegetable to look like a whale's nipple in **Nourish**, or using a black bakelite telephone as a periscope in **Persicope and Sheet Music** is daunting, to say the least. (But are we really so certain what a whale's nipple looks like? Are we certain we could recognise a periscope at such close range? It is true that Horace Walpole was startled by a metal wig worn by Lady Mary Wortley Montagu's mad son, but in this case truth may be stranger than fiction.) Abstract values take care of themselves in this process. Webb's need to make deflections, complications, within a unitary meaning proves as strong as his desire to mix media, to employ words, to be honest to the confusion of events and the particularity of objects. His belief in obtrusive detail proceeds from an almost truculent need to fend for himself, to start from scratch again and again, coping with what comes to hand, like the explorer to whom his work pays homage. For 'perversity' read 'ingenuity'. And operating with cheap props in a small studio with an old-fashioned camera comes under the same heading. Part of the development of Boyd Webb's mature style lay in taking the limitations imposed on him and making them into the conventions of his art. What could be more honest?

'A certain kind of moral uprightness' is how

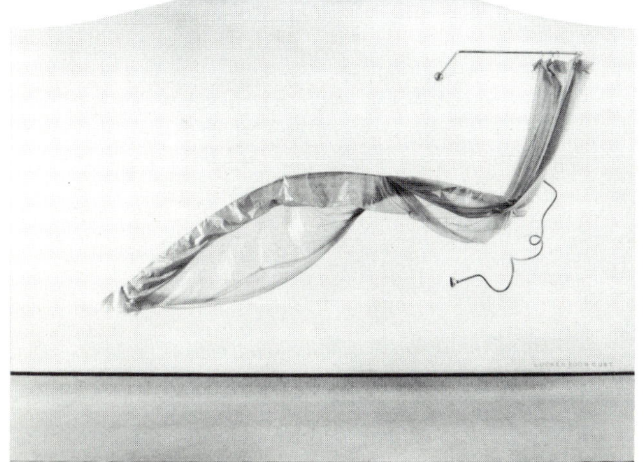

7. **Pink Curtain,** 1979
Colour photograph
50 × 35 cms

Webb has described his approach. The phrase can be applied to his technique, in particular. One late 1960s term, 'arte povera', was coined to describe a return to simple forms, gestures and materials. Webb's postwar 'poverty' takes a different tack. His approach has a lot in common with Do-It-Yourself, not only an attempt to resist professionalism but also a plan to circumvent it entirely. So a set of props can be recycled; **Locker Room Gust** (fig. 6) and **Pink Curtain** (fig. 7), for example, consist of the same pink curtain twisted into different shapes, while some sequences continue to play with the same configurations for as long as possible. They can be considered as groups, without any internal chronology. (One group would contain **Subcontinent**, **Survey**, and **Red Shoes**.) As objects recur, so do people. Indeed, the whole internal economy of Webb's work revolves around what exists, can be found, retrieved or made in

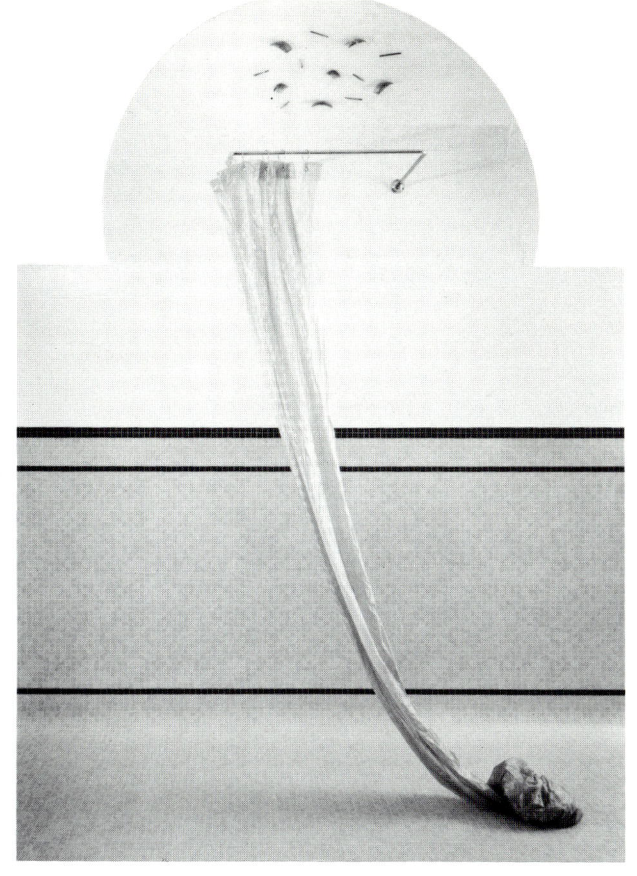

6. **Locker Room Gust,** 1980
Colour photograph
50.5 × 40 cms

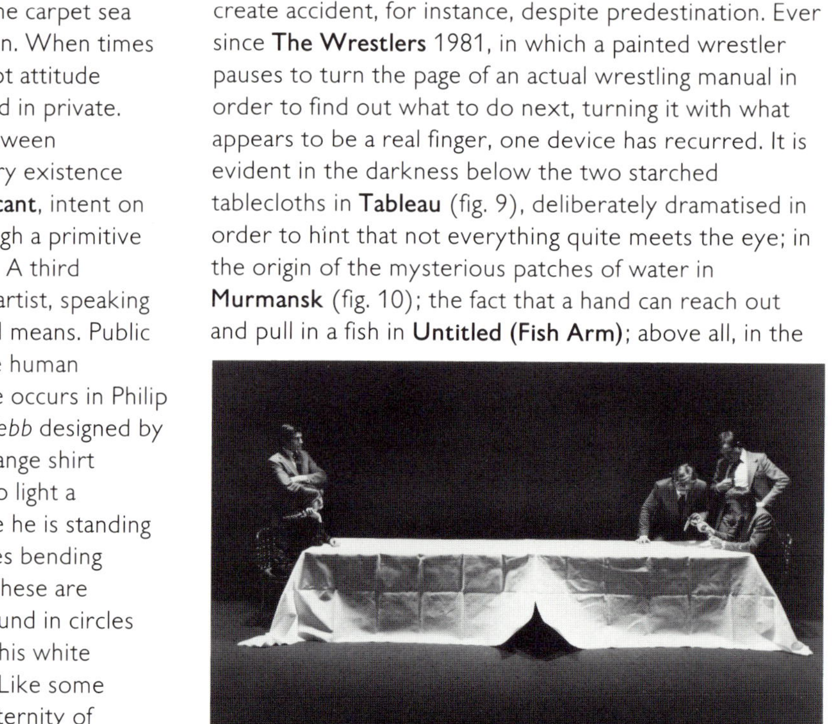

8. **The Mandatory Second Opinion,** 1978
    Colour photograph
    29 × 37.5 cms

or around his studio. Indian vegetables occur, for example, because they can be bought easily in the area where he works. But his best coinages – the underlay, the paper sky with flung paint for stars, the carpet sea and linoleum rocks – occur again and again. When times are hard, he implies, a waste-not-want-not attitude passes for morality, a virtue best practised in private. Public uprightness emerges as a cross between interference and sheer masochism. Its very existence causes confusion. Is the woman in **Supplicant**, intent on addressing a non-existent audience through a primitive paper megaphone, a heroine or a lunatic? A third possibility exists: she could simply be an artist, speaking to an invisible audience by using outdated means. Public uprightness seems a necessary part of the human condition. One classic case of forbearance occurs in Philip Haas's film *Scenes and Songs from Boyd Webb* designed by Webb himself. A man wearing only an orange shirt tucked into his white underpants needs to light a cigarette but finds this impossible because he is standing on a revolving dais. In desperation, he tries bending forward to reach two lighted tapers, but these are mounted on two toy tanks which run around in circles between his legs, their flames so close to his white underpants that they leave a smoky trail. Like some latterday Prometheus, he undergoes an eternity of punishment, torn between two choices – lighting a cigarette and singeing his private parts. His only possible option is to go on.

Human helplessness also extends to

intellectual matters. Webb has little sympathy for measurers and makers of rules, partly because their perception seems so limited, partly because events are too strange to predict. A key reference for his work is the Sufi tale of the blind men and the elephant, each feeling a single part, then reporting back to the others about a completely different animal from the one they suppose they are touching. His Bouvard and Pécuchet equivalents in **The Mandatory Second Opinion** (fig. 8) also argue about elephants, in this case the shape of elephants' heads, each seeing the shape of his own instead. Perhaps Webb's view of these men and related scholars like **The Strategist** is understandable. Classic English hymns harp on the idea of the largeness of God's comprehension in comparison to that of Man, who is weak-willed and incapable of seeing beyond his nose. In his own private universe Webb is God and his attitude to those who try to think their way out of their position is not always a kindly one. After all, he himself is restricted enough.

Webb had already considered issues of control. If gods exist, they must have the power to create accident, for instance, despite predestination. Ever since **The Wrestlers** 1981, in which a painted wrestler pauses to turn the page of an actual wrestling manual in order to find out what to do next, turning it with what appears to be a real finger, one device has recurred. It is evident in the darkness below the two starched tablecloths in **Tableau** (fig. 9), deliberately dramatised in order to hint that not everything quite meets the eye; in the origin of the mysterious patches of water in **Murmansk** (fig. 10); the fact that a hand can reach out and pull in a fish in **Untitled (Fish Arm)**; above all, in the

9. **Tableau,** 1978
    Colour photograph
    56 × 76.5 cms

powers of artistic creation; the idea of two interconnected parts, whether words or pictures, a pair of characters or a double unit of meaning, common enough in his previous work, is seen here as a vision of doom.

Perhaps it is odd that by the 1980s Webb's universe seems to have gathered a momentum of its own, despite the dependence on what comes to hand, the outdated machinery and the dogged refusal to alter the evidence it provides. All that is needed is the kind of husbandry featured in *Scenes and Songs*, where humans are seen as slaves, keeping geese alive. The film is an extended attempt to forge links between various elements of his system, and provides clues to the relationship between the parts of his fictional world and its internal workings. It proves to be a place where waste and value exist in a self-regulating system which operates of its own accord. Food, for example, is never wasted; it simply turns into a regenerative agent and as such deserves to be prized. So a work called **Provisions** shows rotten vegetables which have sunk beneath ice-floes, while **Guano** (fig. 12) drops like manna onto a tiny living-room table way below. Broken eggs turn into solar volcanoes in *Scenes and Songs*, a veritable hymn to dairy produce, after which, almost of its own accord, the world of Boyd Webb switches from beginnings to endings.

Devoid of figures, his subsequent cycles were based on ideas of survival. From one point of view they resemble an apocalyptic vision which looks forward to the possible abandonment of the entire planet. Images of Noah's ark combine with those of science-fiction.

10. **Murmansk,** 1981
Colour photograph
106.5 × 76 cms

hint that a blank plane can be identified with the screen in a cinema, or the canvas in a painting, and that a presence might well exist behind such an innocent surface. These all suggest a ghost in the machine, more like a stowaway than a ship's captain, capable of partly revealing himself in order to hint that although it may be all his own work, he does not relish the degree of sovereignty he has over it. A self-portrait made for *Beaux-Arts* magazine in 1984 shows Webb as Atlas, taking the strain of a carpet globe, but eavesdropping as he does so, as if removed from his creation, he remains curious about what happens to it. Images of creation are however offset by intimations of apocalypse, **Relics of a Day of Reckoning** (fig. 11) shows two grotesque fish in the act of devouring each other against the background of a ruined city beneath the sea, purchased from an aquarium shop and mounted on linoleum. This simultaneous destruction of civilisations and mutual cannibalism suggests the eventual downfall of his own

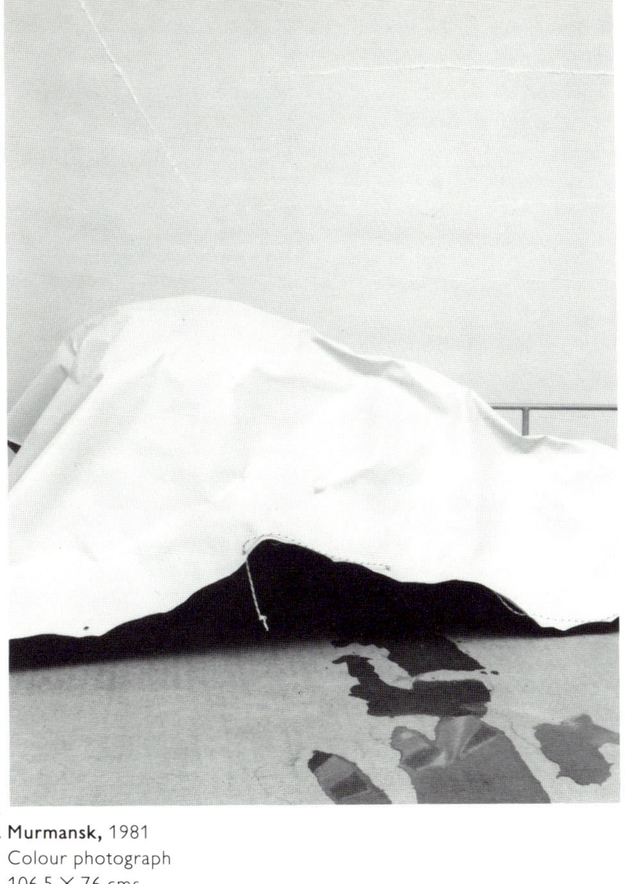

11. **Relics of a Day of Reckoning,** 1980
Colour photograph
38 × 49 cms

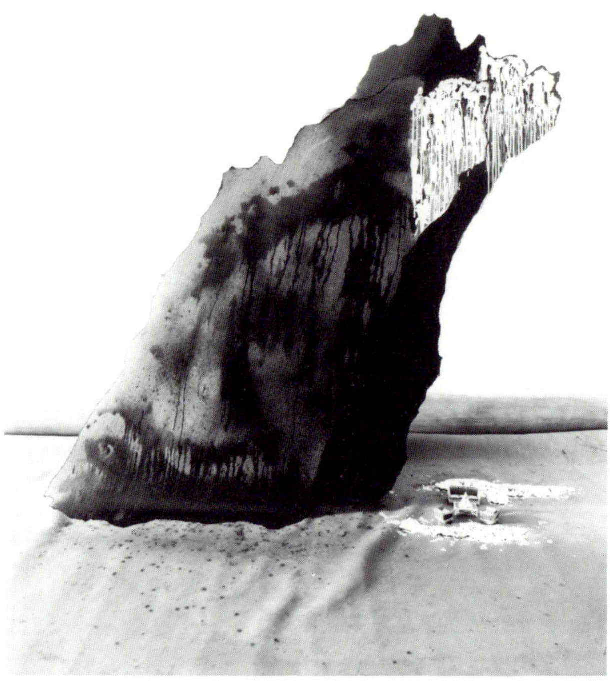

12. **Guano,** 1981
Colour photograph
101 X 79 cms

Renounce shows paraphernalia which cannot be taken on board while **First Principles** focuses on necessities – an electric toaster and a ball of knitting, which dangle from a passing spacecraft. Civilisation must be continued at all costs; in **Kibbutz** a man reads Braille with his tongue in order to help him fashion models of agricultural machinery, as if he had undergone a mutation and needed to learn how to create all over again. Ends are confused with beginnings. Mankind goes naked in space, in a state of prehistoric simplicity, like the family in **Bedding**. Yet people themselves fade from view as the series continues. Suddenly it seems that machines have taken on a life of their own, even, in **Cupid's Sting**, a sex-life, impregnating each other at long distance. Webb's outer space recalls his submarine period, but with new potential for illusions of distance and weightlessness. If distance is one main concern, so is substance itself; Webb is intent on simulating space and even black holes. (Predictably, *his* black hole gapes to reveal slices of fruit cake.) By the mid 1980s Webb has reached his most distant horizon. If each stage of his career provides a test

and an extension of his running concerns, this is the most completely self-involved of those stages, with chronological time coming full-circle and the images referring more and more to their own states of existence. Increasingly, these are works about the making of a fictional world, in one case about the very creation of one before our eyes. As a globe develops a spiralling fault like apple peel falling away, a primitive head appears, like a new model of a human being. A spiral of paper is enough to signify a Chernobyl-style meltdown of an entire planet. Yet the postcard of the Cycladic head makes **Glorious Morning** an optimistic work after all. At points like this Webb demonstrates his ability to speak in his own terms about fundamental human mysteries, contemplated, not solved, with their strangeness left intact.

The acceptance of a cosmology, at once the concept and visual image of a world-view, is now so commonplace that it goes unmentioned. Part myth, part fault, part fact, a 'world picture' summarises the state of belief current at any time. In an age of electron microscopes and subatomic physics, of quarks and supernovae, the mere idea of a cosmology might seem impossible. Yet daily physics or biology proves quite different from the version scientists discuss.

The late 1960s and early 1970s, Webb's point of emergence as an artist, coincided with two debates in other media, both relevant in considering his contribution to larger debates. The first was the coining of the term 'metafiction' by the American philosopher and novelist William Gass in 1970 and the second was the publication of Peter L. Berger and Thomas Luckmann's *The Social Construction of Reality* in 1971. While Webb has tried to rid his work of linear plot, he has nevertheless retained the conditions surrounding that plot: the state of suspended belief, the air of charade which passes for shoestring theatre, but goes beyond it by employing a repertory of actors, a repertoire of props, the atmosphere of the 'tableau vivant'. By insisting on the identical gesture which characterises 'metafiction' and demands that suffix 'meta-', the act of establishing the conventions of fiction then laying them bare, he offers his viewers a lie which they accept in a spirit of play, as a lie. Acceptance of the exposure of levels of illusion and acceptance of play as play can mean arming oneself against the bogus definitions of play which contemporary life presents to the unwary, a refining of a sensibility which is simultaneously moral and aesthetic. But, as Berger and Luckmann argue, 'reality' as we know it consists of a set of intersecting realities among which the everyday version looms largest, and excursions outside it invariably return to this normative basis, or 'paramount reality'.

For this reason, play may slightly alter our notion of reality but will never undermine it. The role of the everyday in Webb's work is inextricably engaged with the excursions into other realities, presented with all the inherent honesty that his Presbyterian upbringing might lead one to expect. Furthermore, his agenda is not predisposed towards idle aestheticism. On the late Elizabethan or Jacobean stage, his equivalent would have been the court masque, brought to its height in the collaboration between Ben Jonson and Inigo Jones. Their entertainments were designed to fulfil a complex brief: an argument in favour of the divine right of kings, set forth, somewhat paradoxically, in the most lavish but transcient way. In keeping with his views on survival as avoidance of conspicuous waste, and the need to compromise in material terms in order to preserve the ever fragile hold on the future of the planet, Webb similarly dramatizes the fate of the figure whom he sees

as responsible. However, his protagonist is not royalty but the average man leading an everyday life. Concentrating on his petty failures in a way that triumphantly copes with parallel failures, Webb says one thing and does another, casting himself honestly and inevitably in the role of God. Some conditions he can do nothing about; one piece, called **Corpse** (fig. 13), shows one of his actors simply lying on the floor with the carpet/earth hanging horizontally above. This kind of inversion needs to be made only once, not as an abdication of responsibility but as a record of where that responsibility ceases, the most serious way of presenting what he has demonstrated elsewhere: that God eats, laughs, makes the occasional mistake, and devises other terms to prevent our catching a glimpse of him. Webb wants his viewers to note all this then half-forget it, to realise that this is not the world but a commentary on the world – the world according to Boyd Webb, less a man than a cottage industry.

Beginning in a room in London his bailiwick has gradually expanded to the highest mountains, the sea-bed, deep space, the far future and the distant past. Secrets of the universe have been explored and a political theory of the responsibility, not for the making but certainly for the sustenance of that universe, has been set forth. Yet, like God Himself, Webb has remained in one place. Where else could he go? Where does he need to go? Never ceasing to call the viewer's attention to the issue of fabrication, the detail becomes one key to unlock the works. His details, unlike those of the Victorians, are apparent 'failures' designed to break the spell that his theatricality is in danger of casting. By however trivial a means, it has to be broken again and again, to show what every Sufi realises, that 'the apparent is the bridge to the real'.

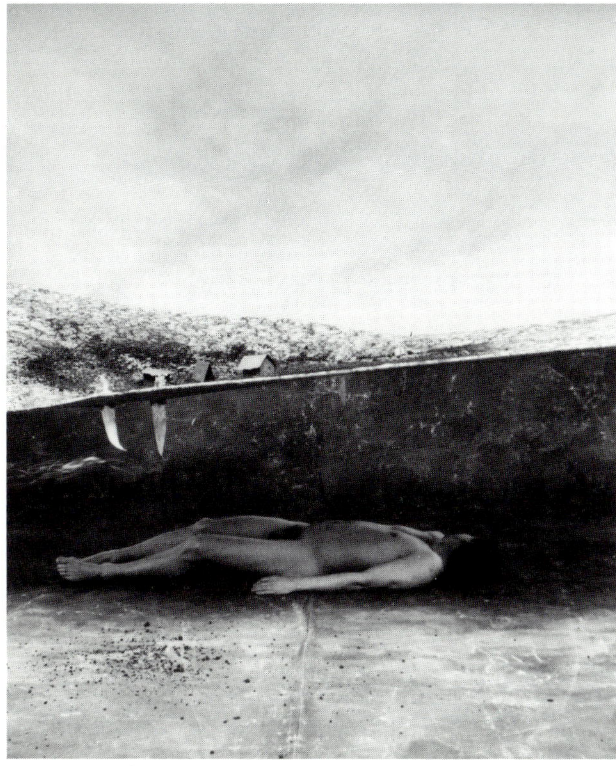

13. **Corpse,** 1983
Colour photograph
40.6 × 30.4 cms

Catalogue

All works are unique colour photographs
Sizes are for unframed works and are given in
centimetres

Untitled (sting ray), 1981
106 × 76.5
Fonds Régional d'Art Contemporain, Lyon

Laurentian, 1981
97 × 77
Collection of the Chase Manhattan Bank

Untitled (fish arm), 1981
78 × 108
Stedelijk Van Abbemuseum, Eindhoven

Untitled (waiter), 1981
63.5 × 89.5
Anthony d'Offay Gallery, London

Untitled (tethered ray), 1981
97 × 71.5
Musée national d'art moderne,
Centre Georges Pompidou, Paris

Bivalve Envy, 1981
67 × 96.5
Musée national d'art moderne,
Centre Georges Pompidou, Paris

Guillemots, 1981
102 × 75.5
Boyd Webb

Survey, 1982
76 × 102
Kunsthaus, Zürich

Nemesis, 1983
115 × 152
Anthony d'Offay Gallery, London

Harvest, 1983
96.5 × 122
Crousel-Hussenot Gallery, Paris

Periscope and Sheet Music, 1983
115 × 151.5
Fundacion Cultural Televisa, Mexico

Shell Shock, 1983
96 × 122
Private collection

Lung, 1983
115 × 152
Anthony d'Offay Gallery, London

Abyssogramme, 1983
152 × 115
Private collection, London

Auto Strafe, 1983
115 × 152
Fonds Régional d'Art Contemporain, Lyon

Postscript, 1983
115 × 152
The Trustees of the Victoria & Albert
Museum, London

Replenish, 1984
153 × 122
City of Salford Art Galleries

Nourish, 1984
152 × 122
Southampton City Art Gallery

Renounce, 1984
152 × 122
Art Gallery of New South Wales, Sydney

Supplicant, 1984
122 × 152
Marlene Wossman, Cologne

Salvage, 1984
122 × 152
Schlumberger Cambridge Research

Tortoise, 1984
119 × 152
Jeanne Meyers, Los Angeles

Strategist, 1984
122 × 152
Anthony d'Offay Gallery, London

Dry Eyed, 1984
122 × 152
Leeds City Art Galleries

Scott's Tent, 1984
122 × 152
The Trustees of the Tate Gallery, London

Provisions, 1984
97 × 152
Anthony d'Offay Gallery, London

Trophy, 1985
122 × 152
Atlantis Museum, Tenerife

Host, 1985
152 × 122
Fonds National d'Art Contemporain, Paris

First Principles, 1985
152 × 122
Crousel-Hussenot Gallery, Paris

Sargasso, 1985
152 × 122
Wendy and Richard Hokin, Connecticut

As Yet Undrawn, 1985
152 × 120
Galerie Schurr, Stuttgart

Kibbutz, 1985
152.5 × 122
Sonnabend Gallery, New York

Sphagnum, 1985
152.5 × 122
Sonnabend Gallery, New York

Clenched, 1985
122 × 152.5
Sonnabend Gallery, New York

Bedding, 1985
122 × 152.5
Sonnabend Gallery, New York

New Rules, 1985
153 × 122
Arts Council of Great Britain

Cupid's Sting, 1986
123 × 154
Fundacion Cultural Televisa, Mexico

Recruit, 1986
152 × 121
Private collection, Athens

Morsel, 1986
121 × 152
Jean Bernier Gallery, Athens

Sprain, 1986
121 × 152
Arrowhead Collection, Athens

Biltong, 1986
121 × 152
Jean Bernier Gallery, Athens

Medallion, 1986
152 × 121
Jean Bernier Gallery, Athens

Glorious Morning, 1986
123 × 154
Edwin C. Cohen, New York

Pupa Rumba Samba, 1986
123 × 154
Williams College Museum of Art,
Williamstown, Massachusetts

Coppice, 1986
154 × 123
Anthony d'Offay Gallery, London

Enzyme, 1987
154 × 123
Karl Bornstein Gallery, Santa Monica

Untitled, 1987
154 × 123
Anthony d'Offay Gallery, London

Coda, 1987
123 × 154
Anthony d'Offay Gallery, London

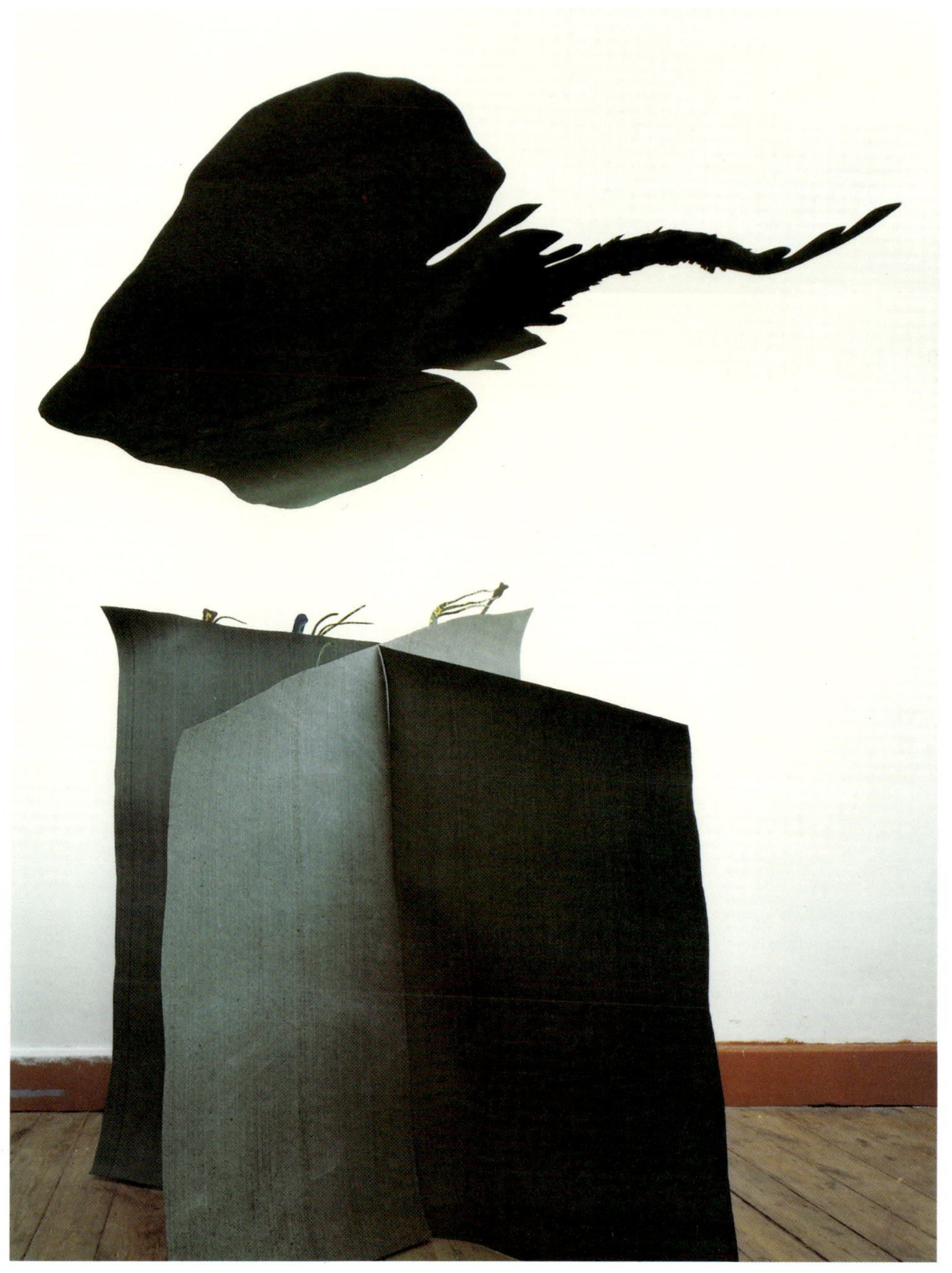

Untitled (sting ray), 1981
106 × 76.5 cms
Fonds Régional d'Art Contemporain, Lyon

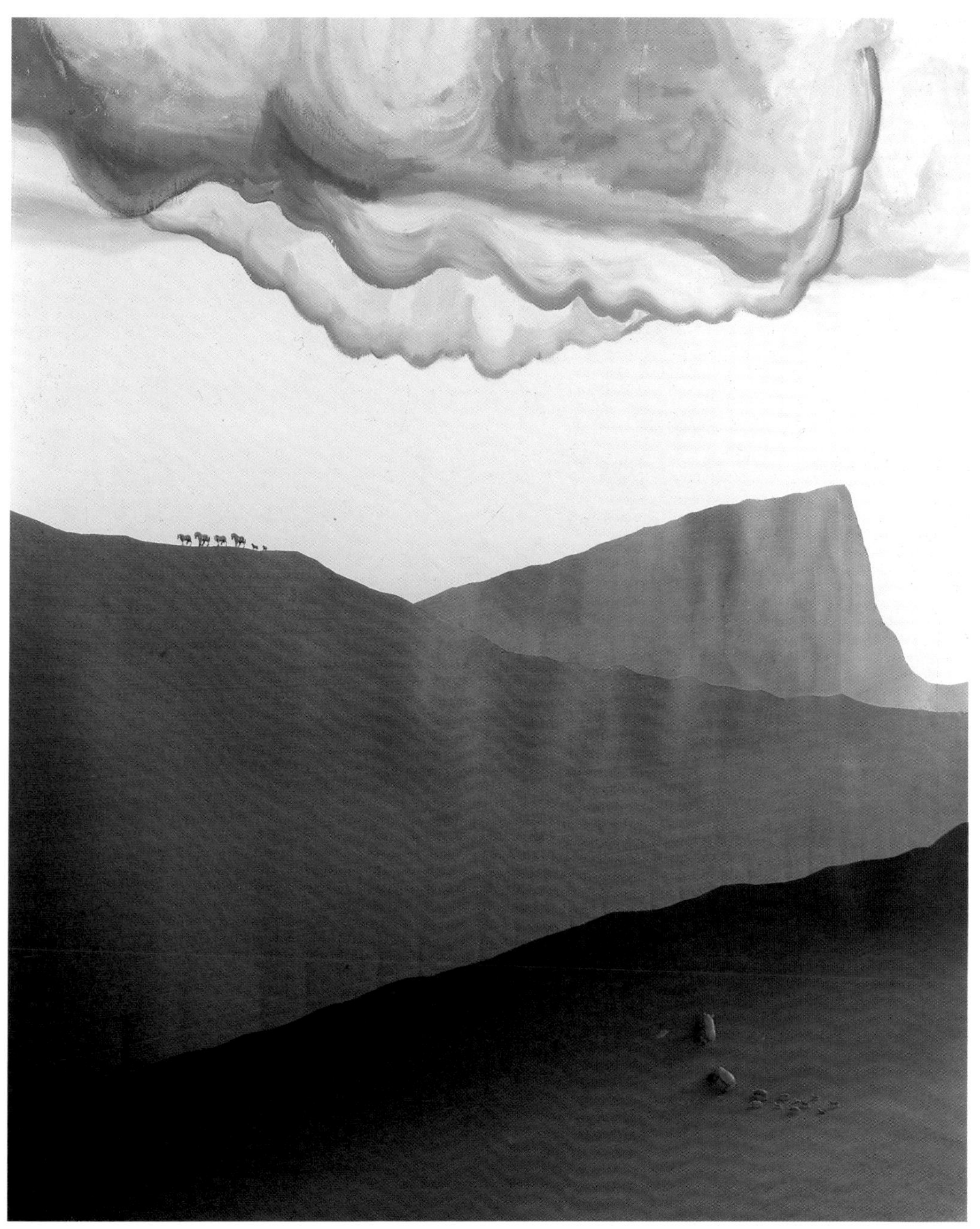

Laurentian, 1981
97 × 77 cms
Collection of the Chase Manhattan Bank

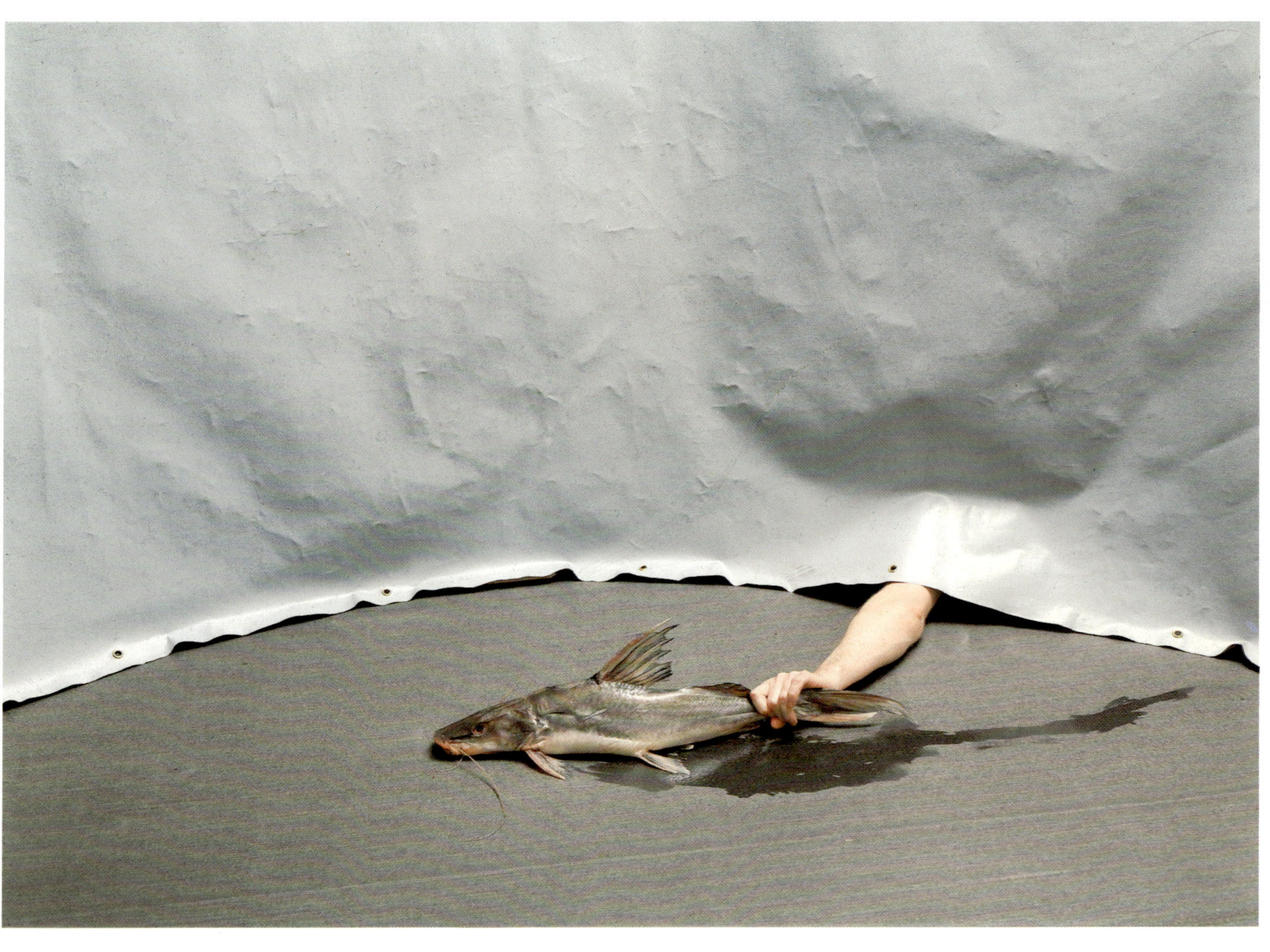

Untitled (fish arm), 1981
78 × 108 cms
Stedelijk Van Abbemuseum, Eindhoven

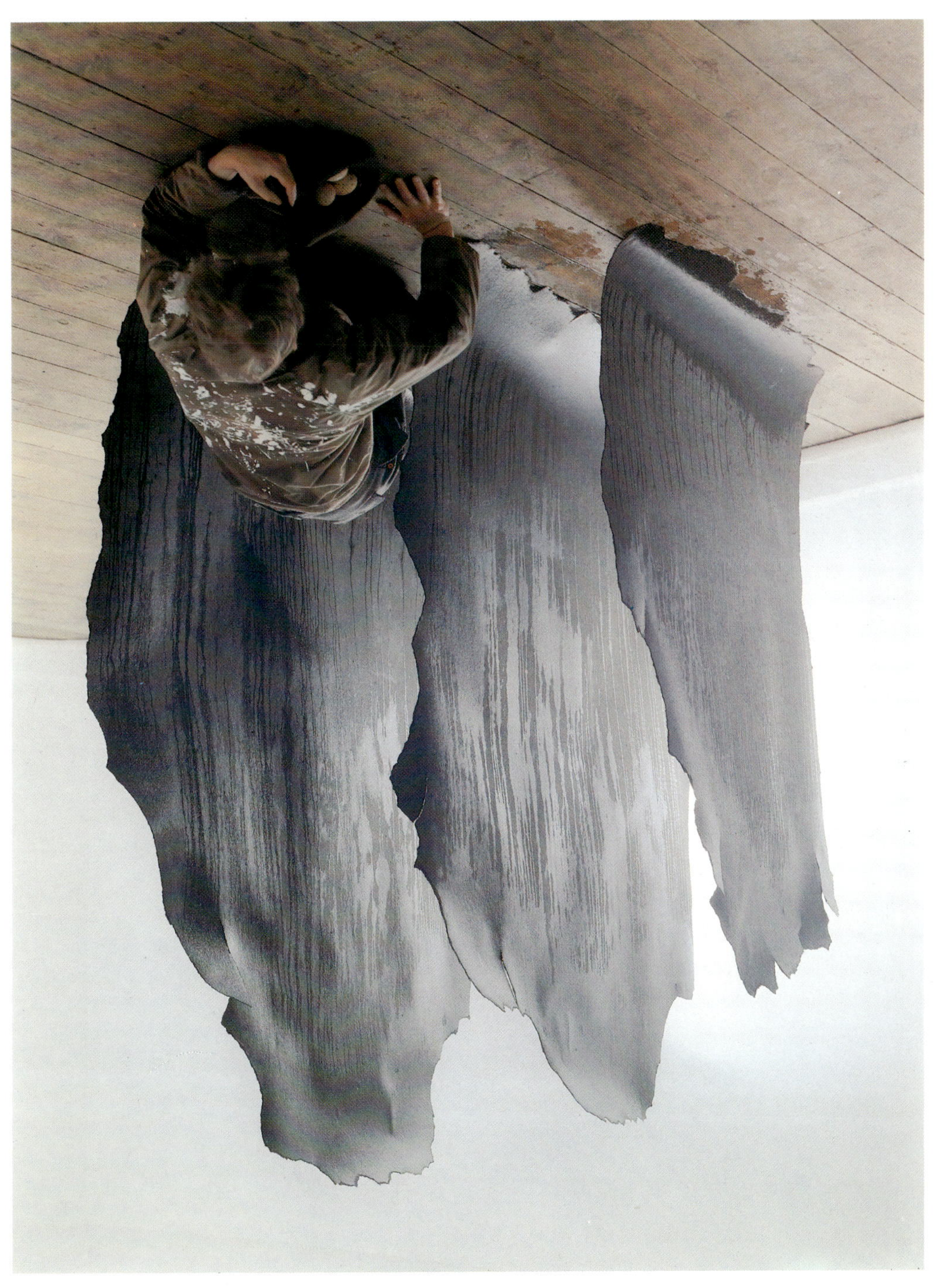

Guillemots, 1981
102 × 75.5 cms
Boyd Webb

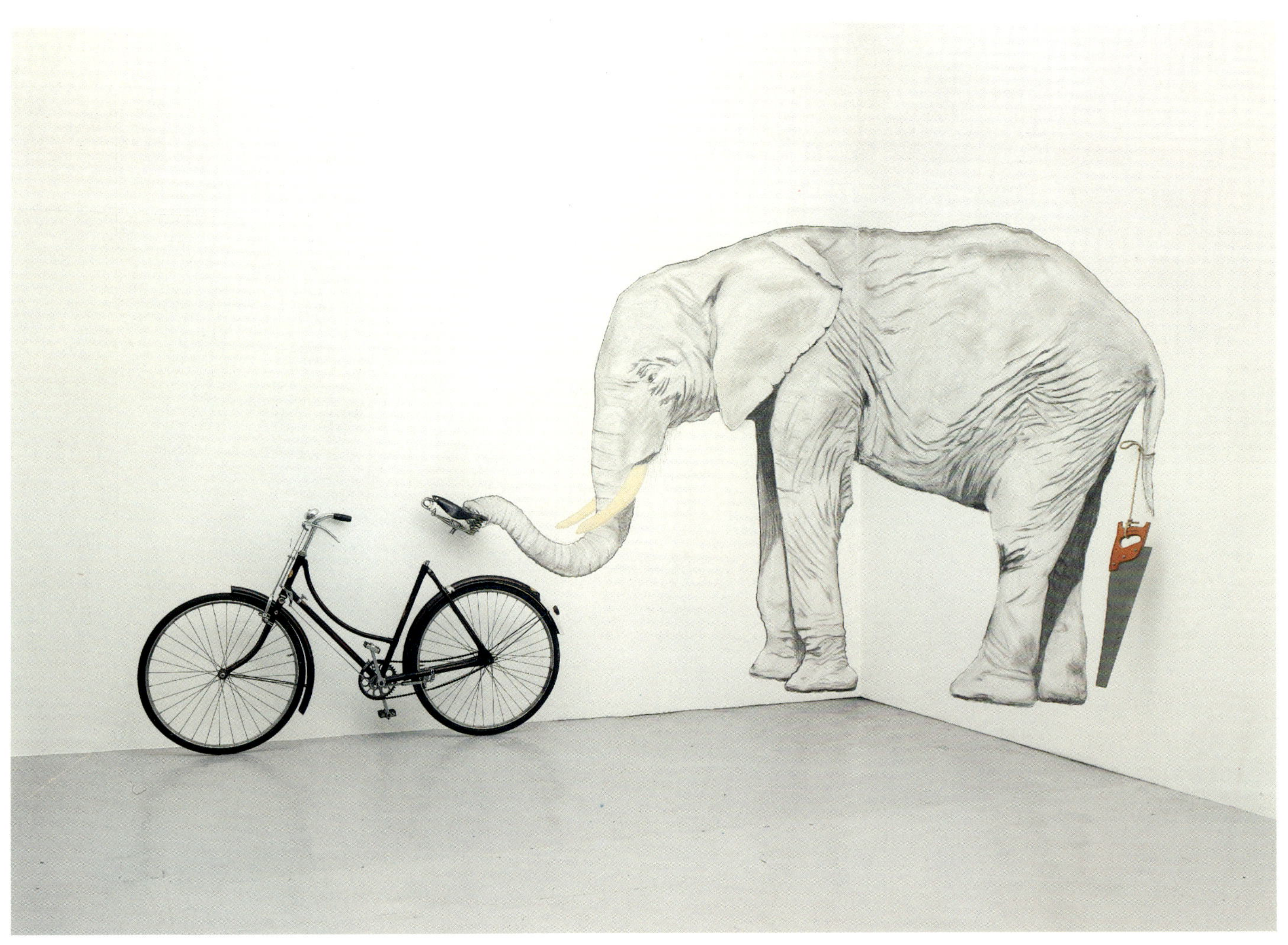

Sub Continent, 1982
76 × 102 cms
Private collection

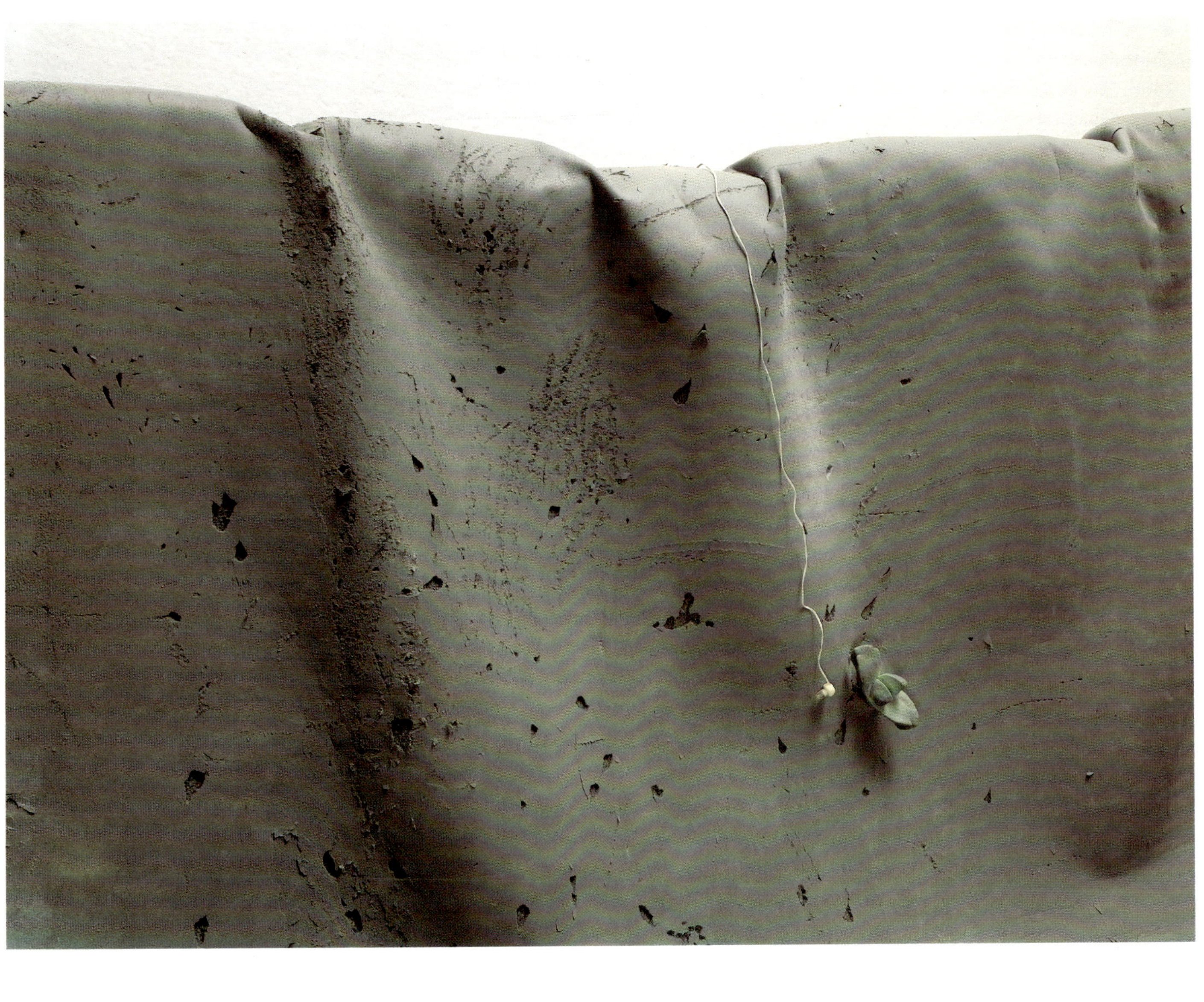

Shell Shock, 1983
96 × 122 cms
Private collection

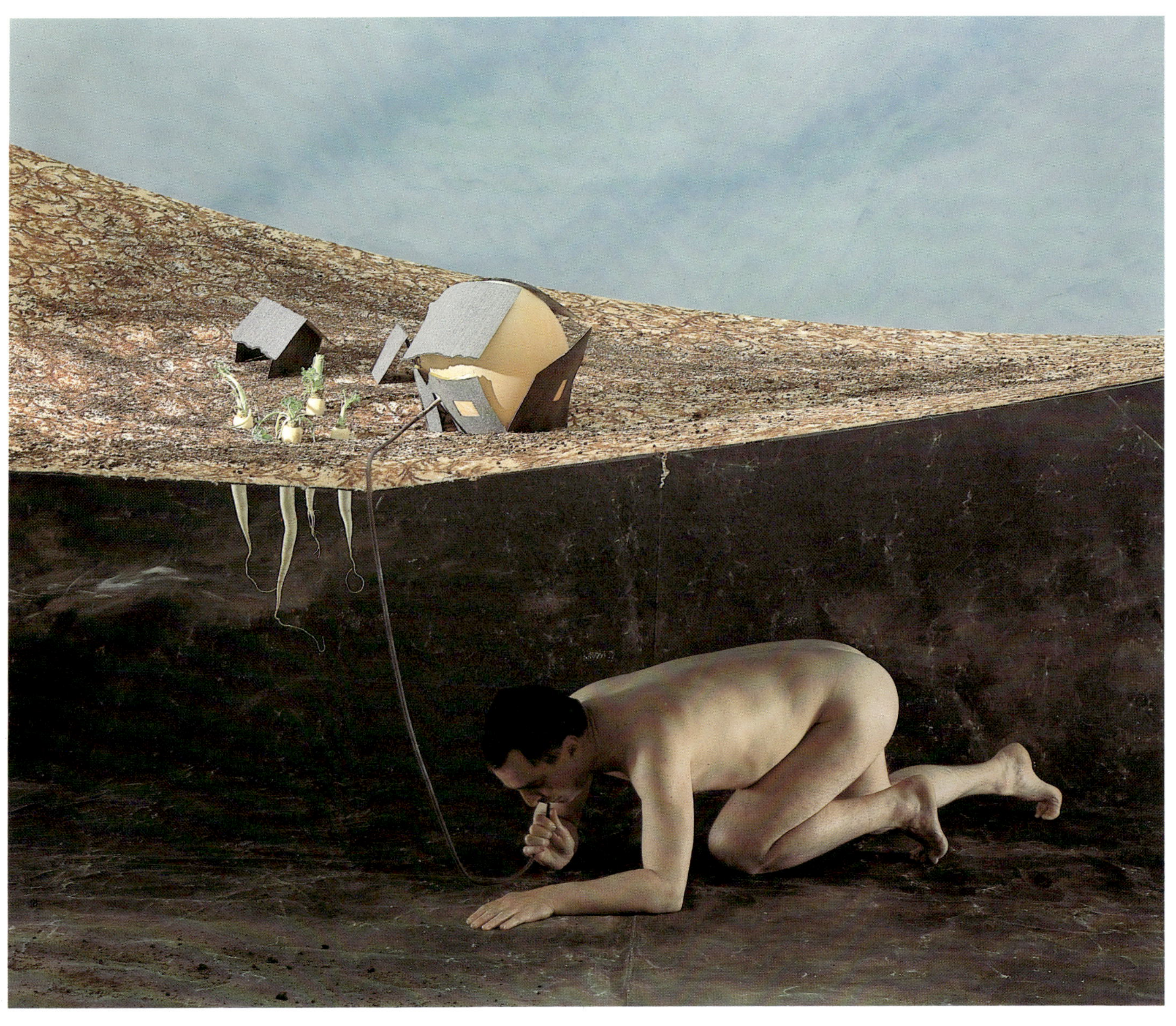

Nemesis, 1983
115 × 152 cms
Anthony d'Offay Gallery, London

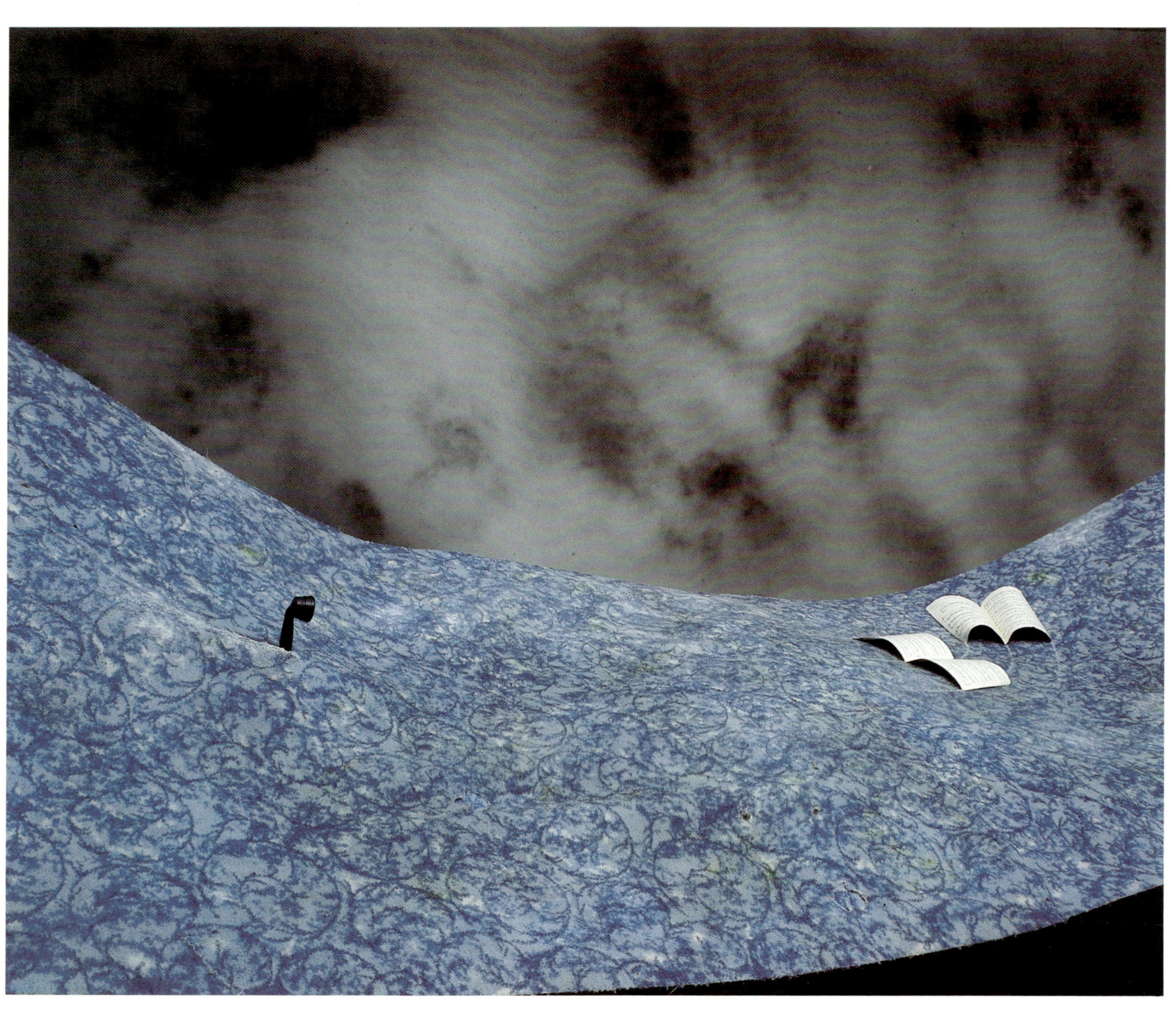

Periscope and Sheet Music, 1983
115 × 151.5 cms
Fundacion Cultural Televisa, Mexico

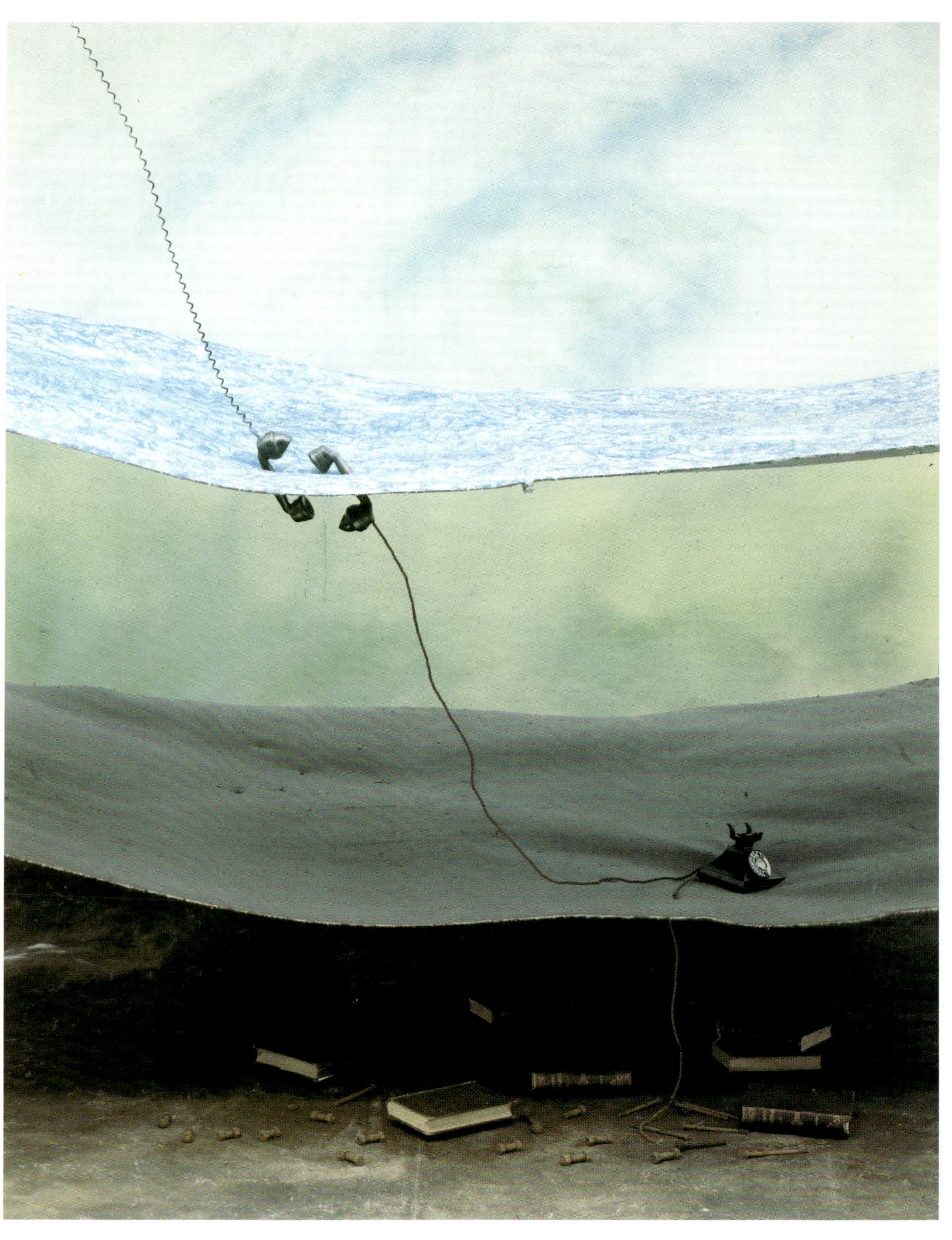

Abyssogramme, 1983
152 × 115 cms
Private collection, London

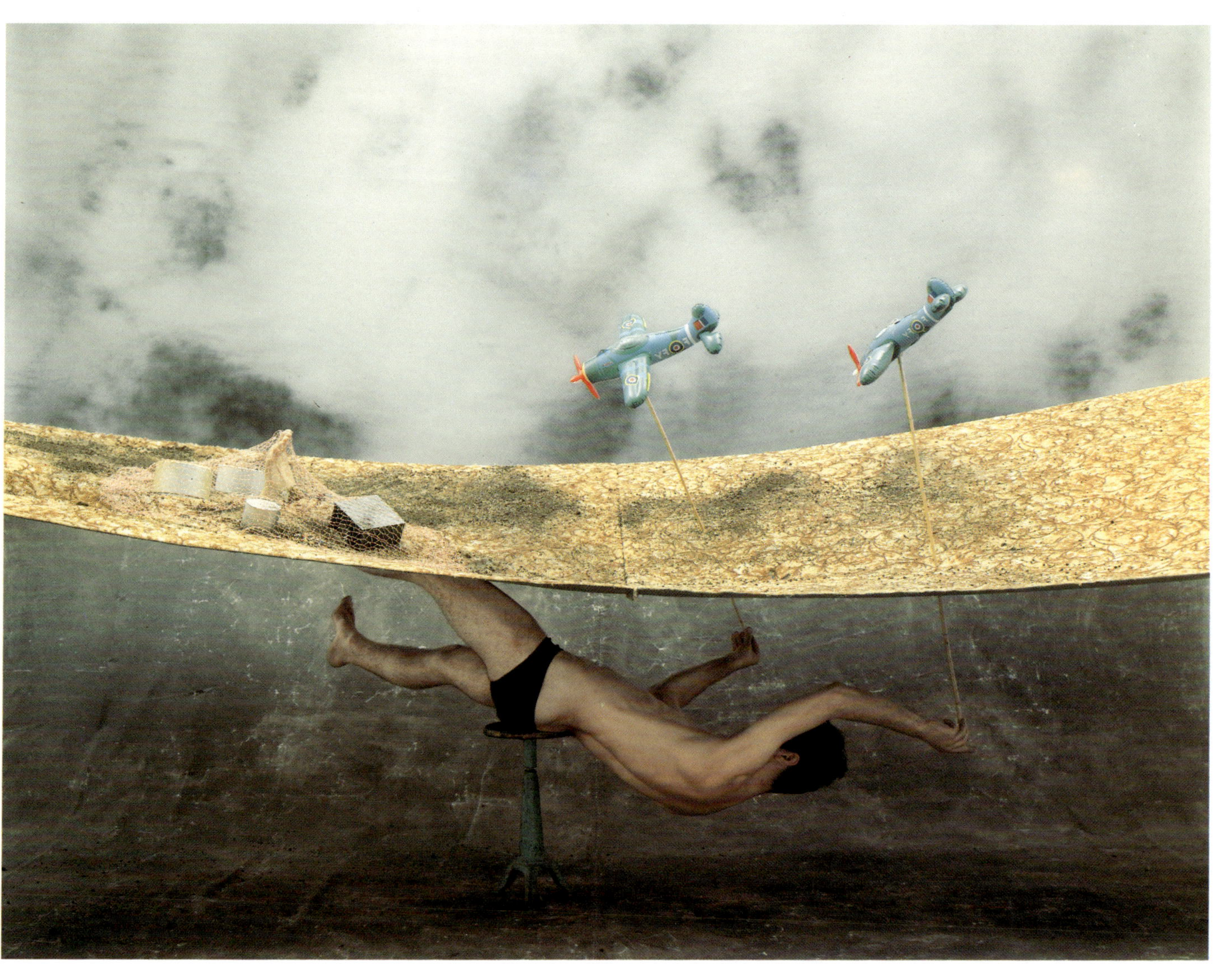

Auto Strafe, 1983
115 × 152 cms
Fonds Régional d'Art Contemporain, Lyon

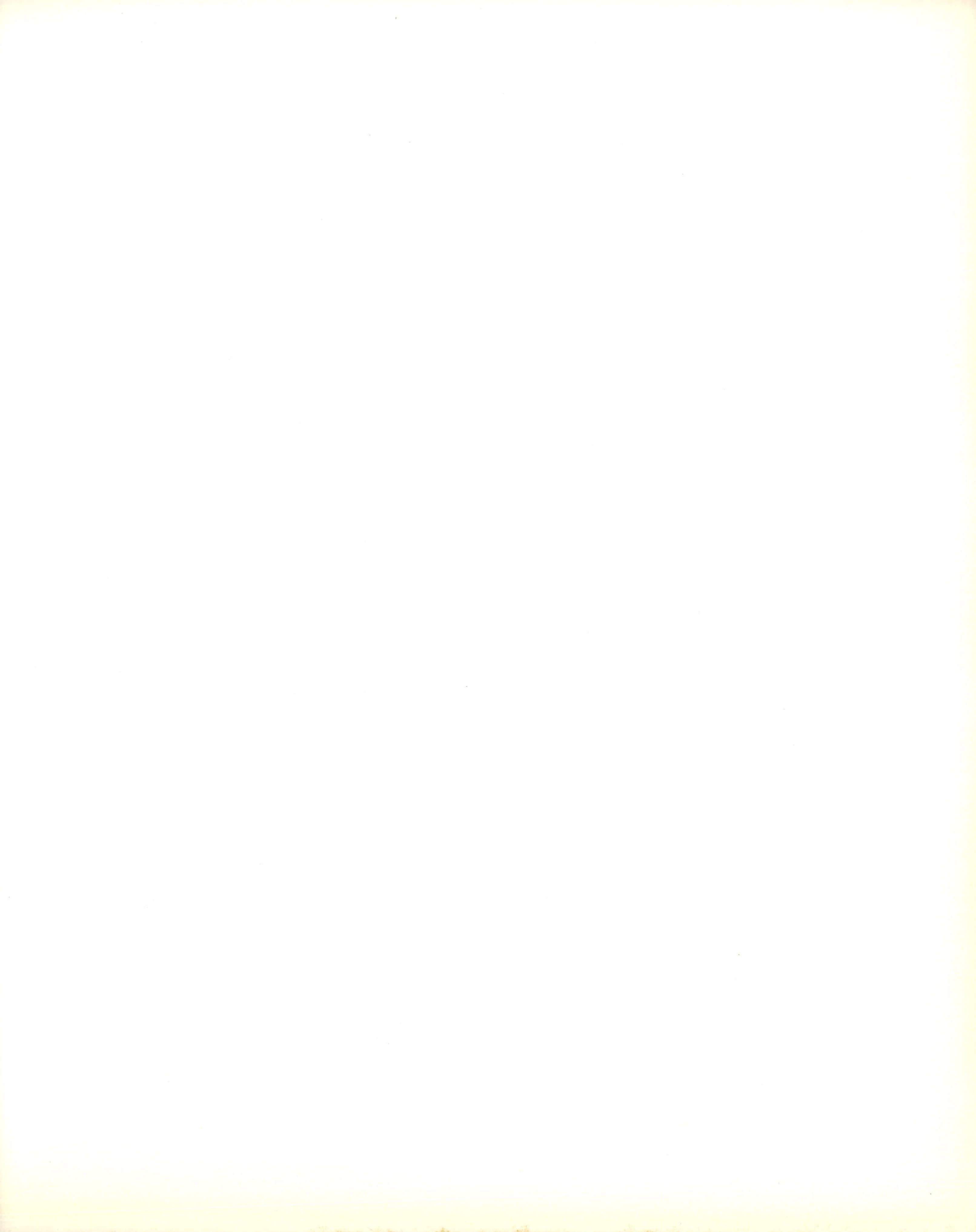

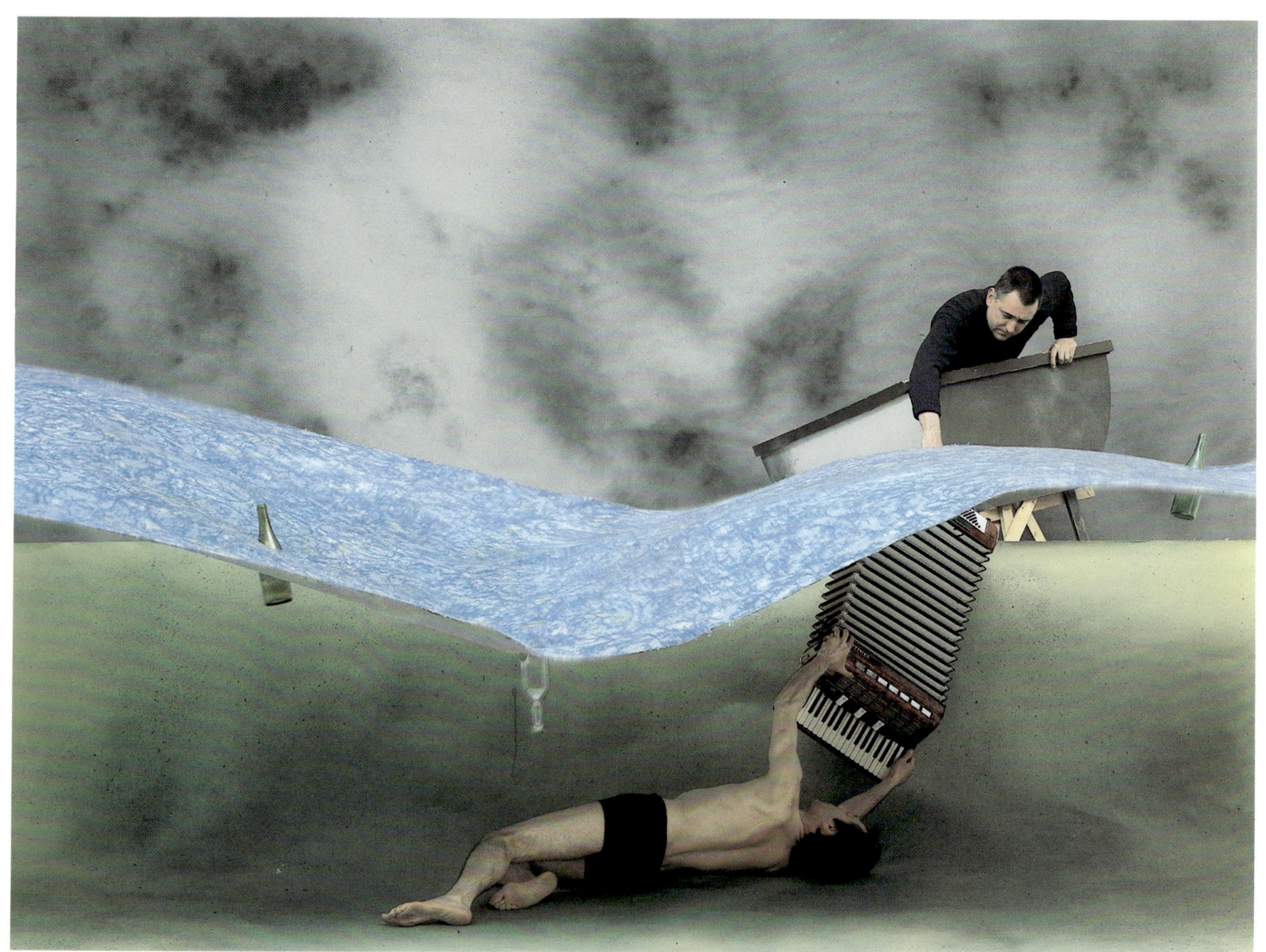

Lung, 1983
115 × 152 cms
Anthony d'Offay Gallery, London

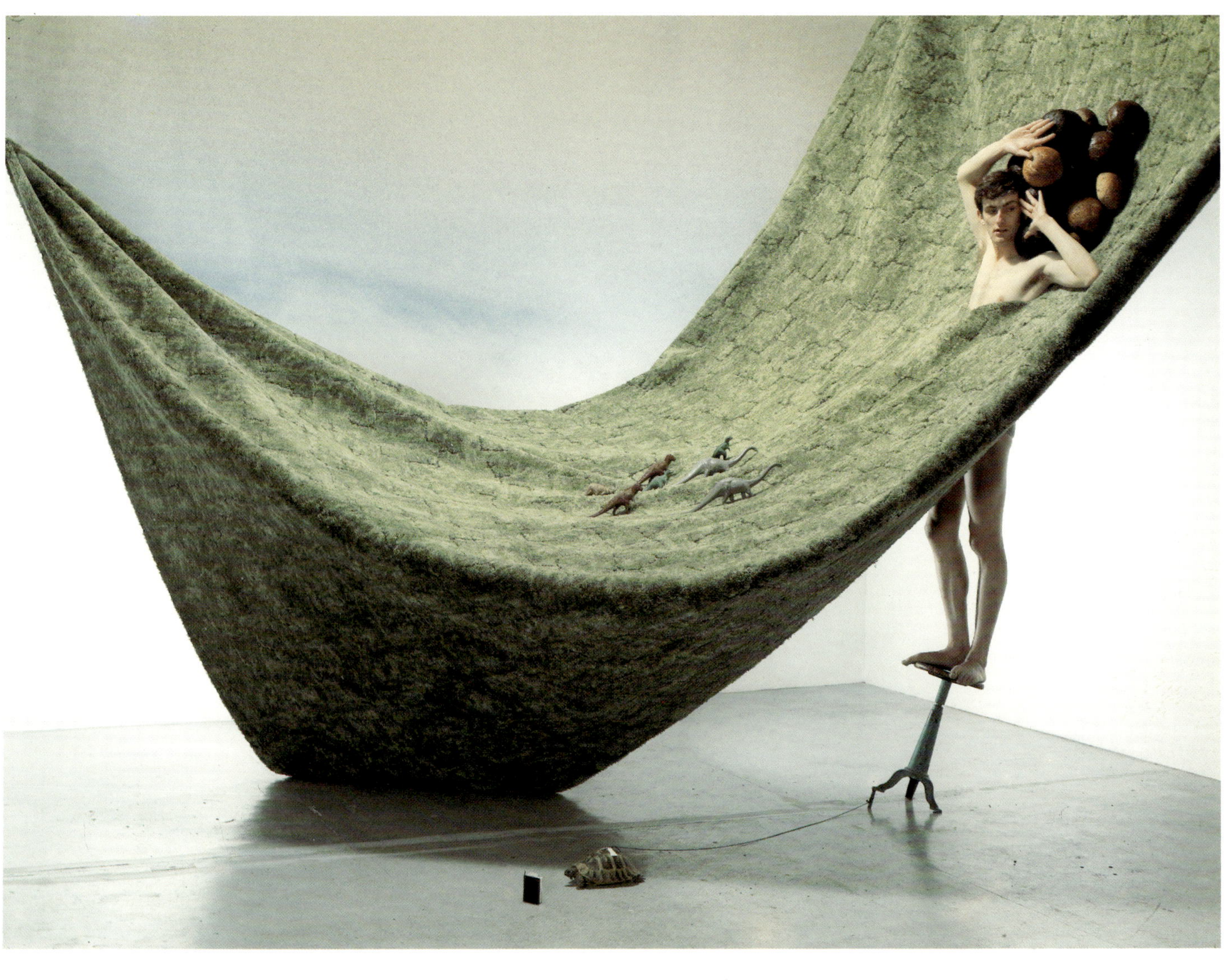

Tortoise, 1984
119 × 152 cms
Jeanne Meyers, Los Angeles

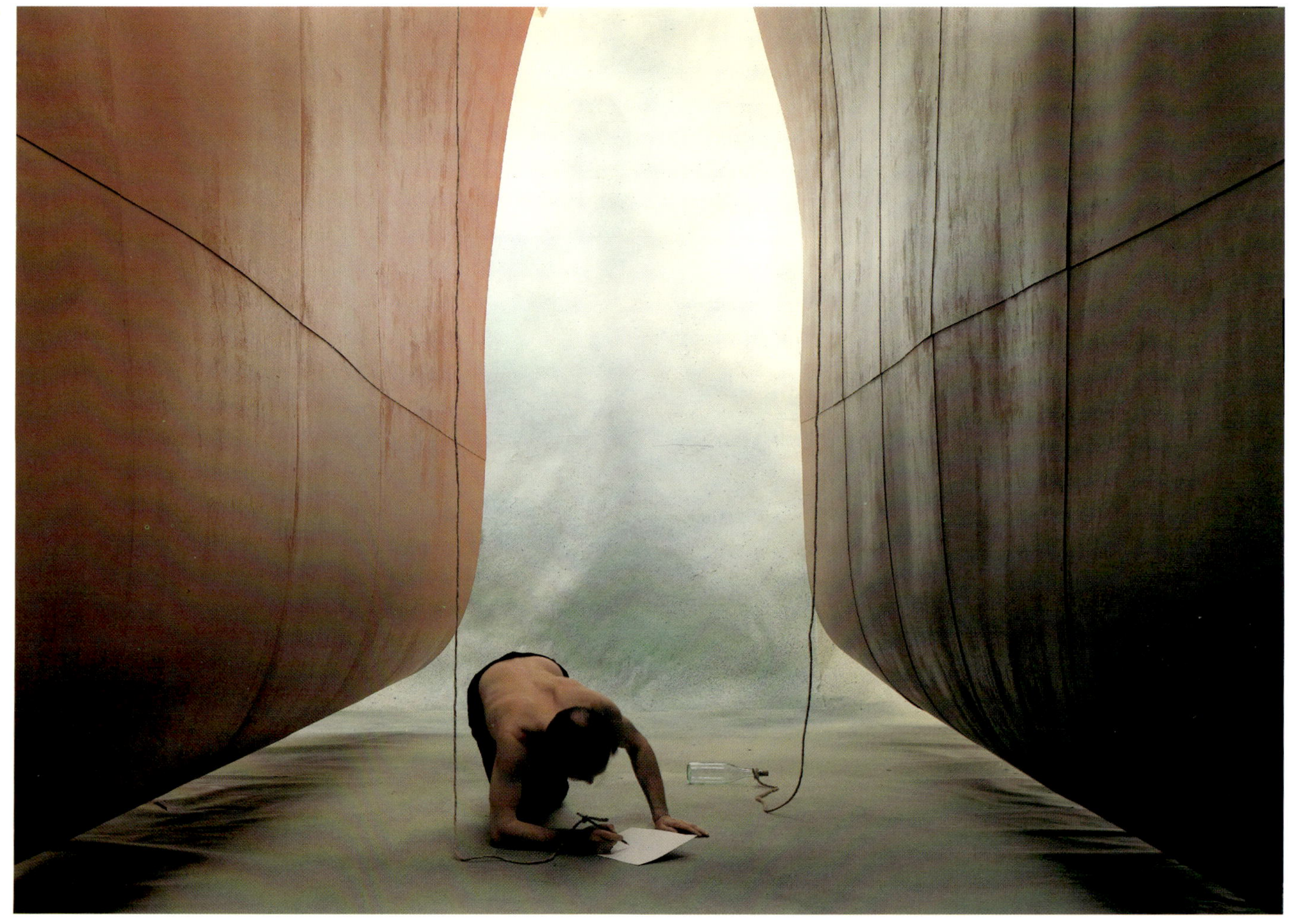

Strategist, 1984
122 × 152 cms
Anthony d'Offay Gallery, London

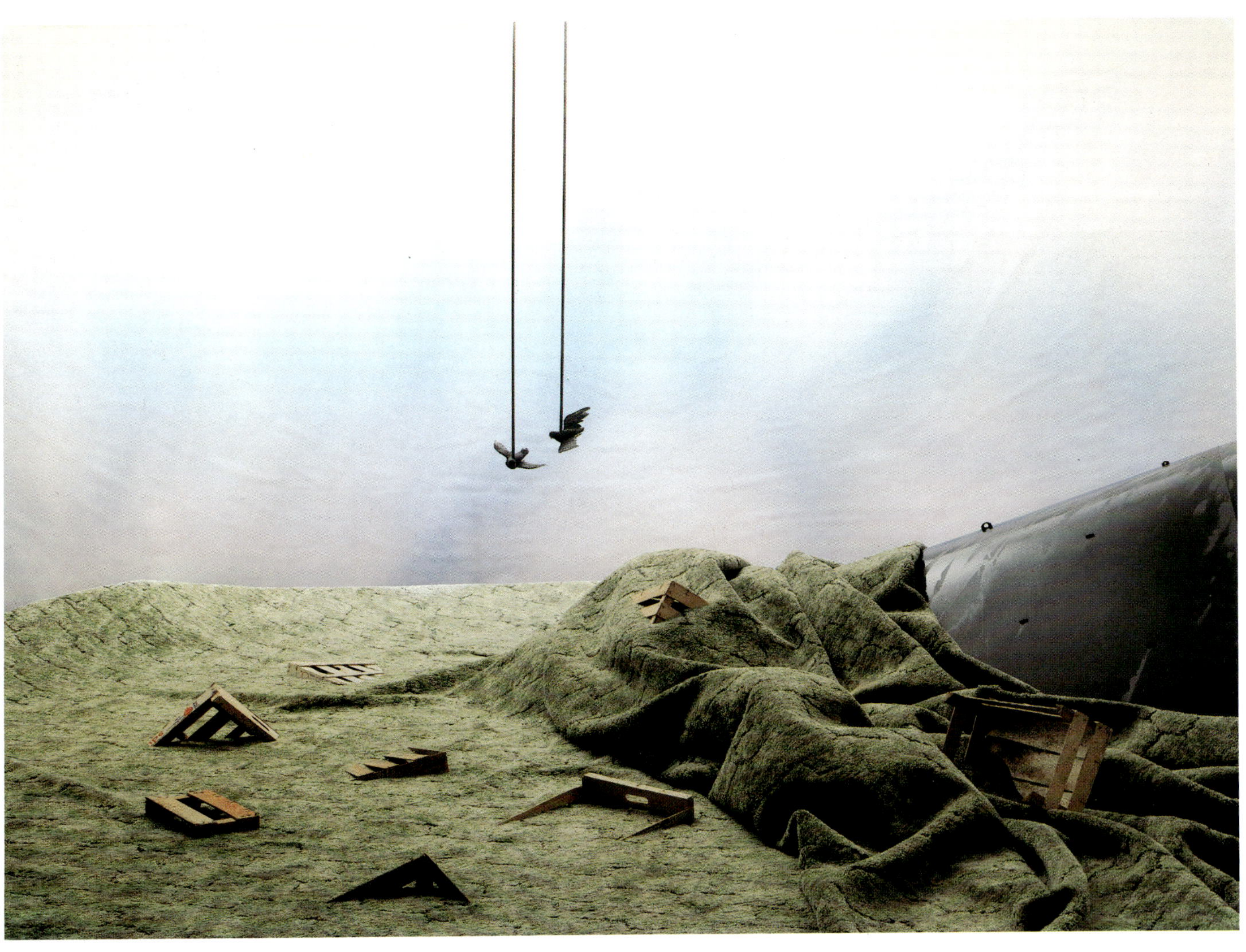

Dry Eyed, 1984
122 × 152 cms
Leeds City Art Galleries

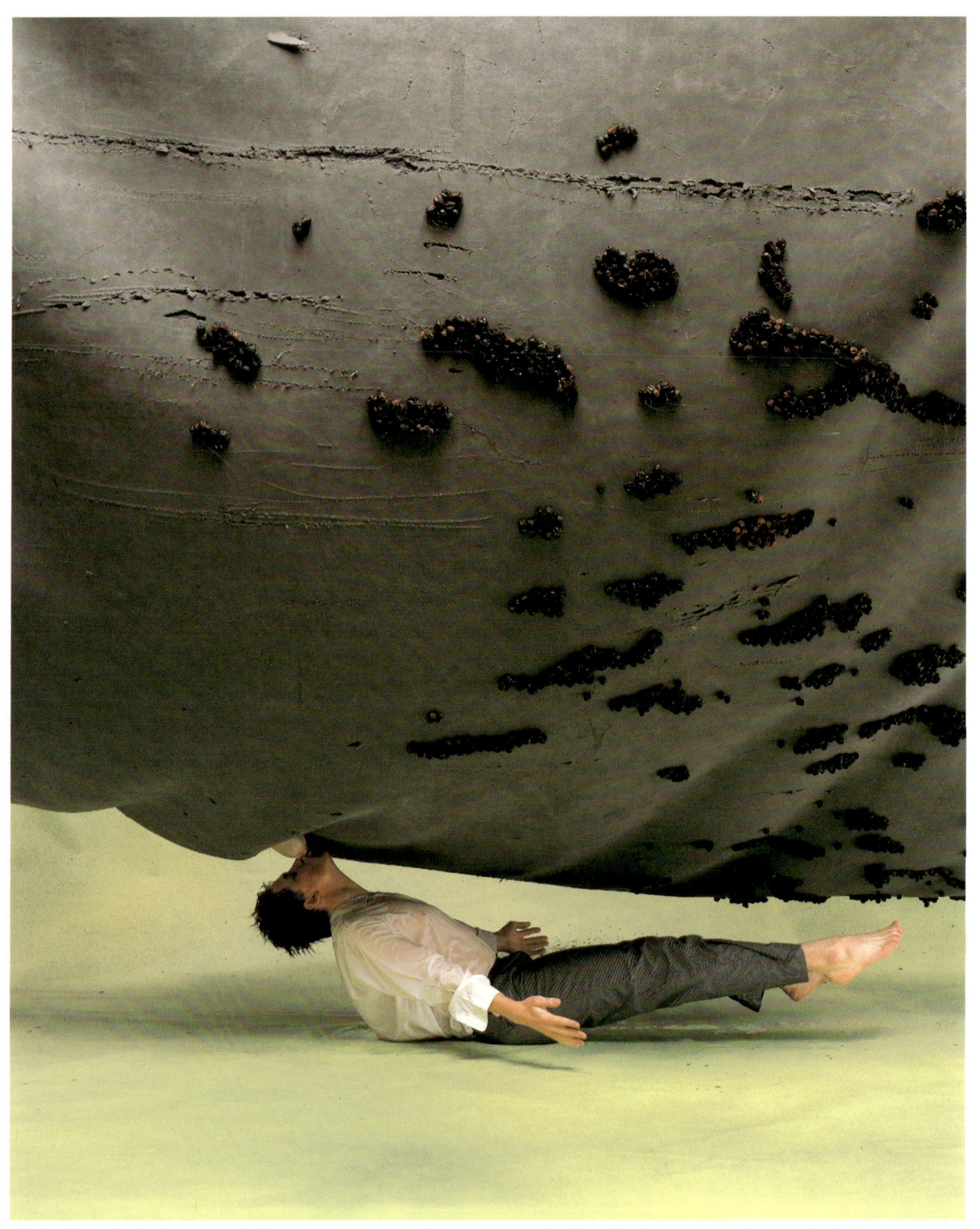

Nourish, 1984
152 × 122 cms
Southampton City Art Gallery

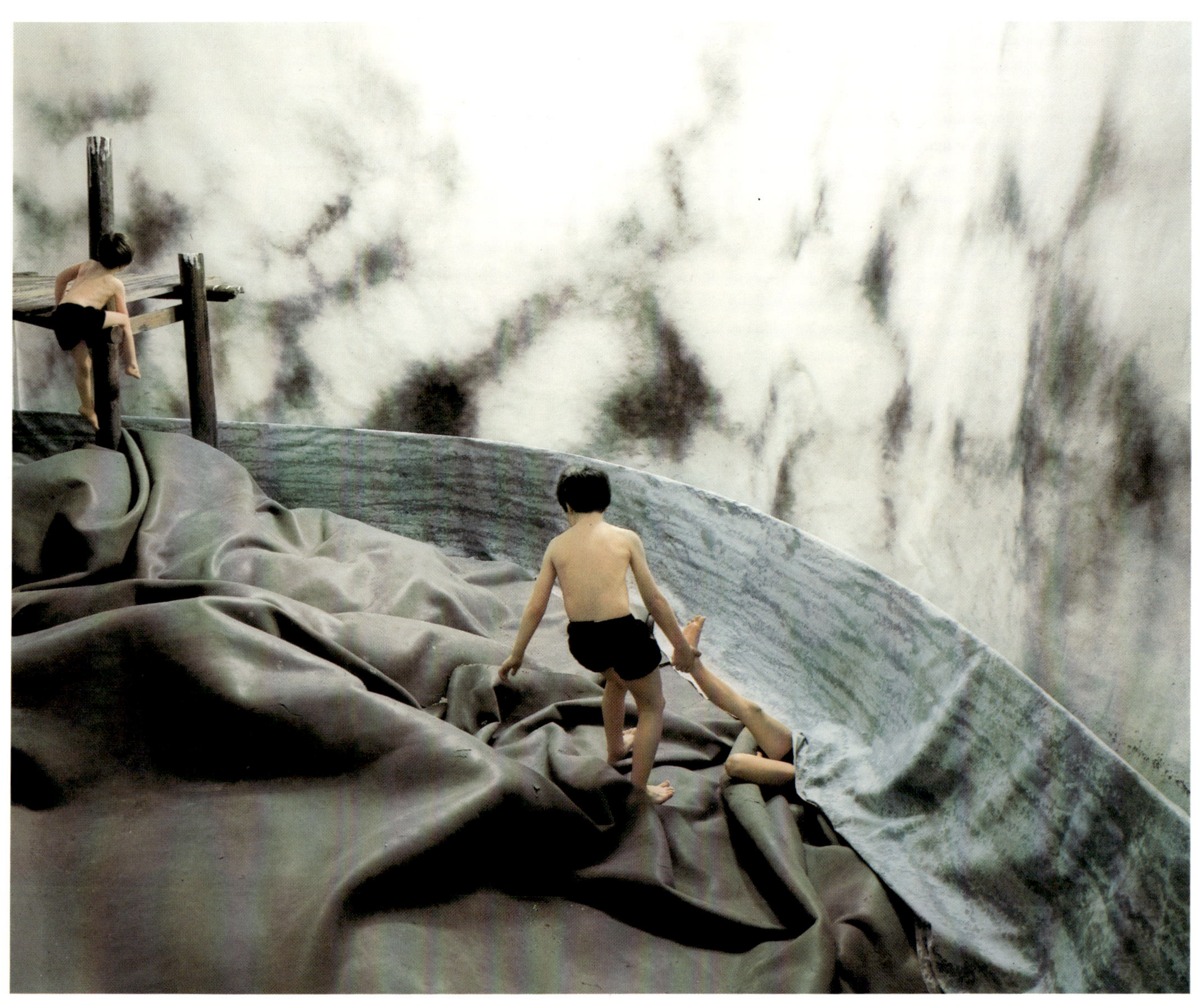

Salvage, 1984
122 × 152 cms
Schlumberger Cambridge Research

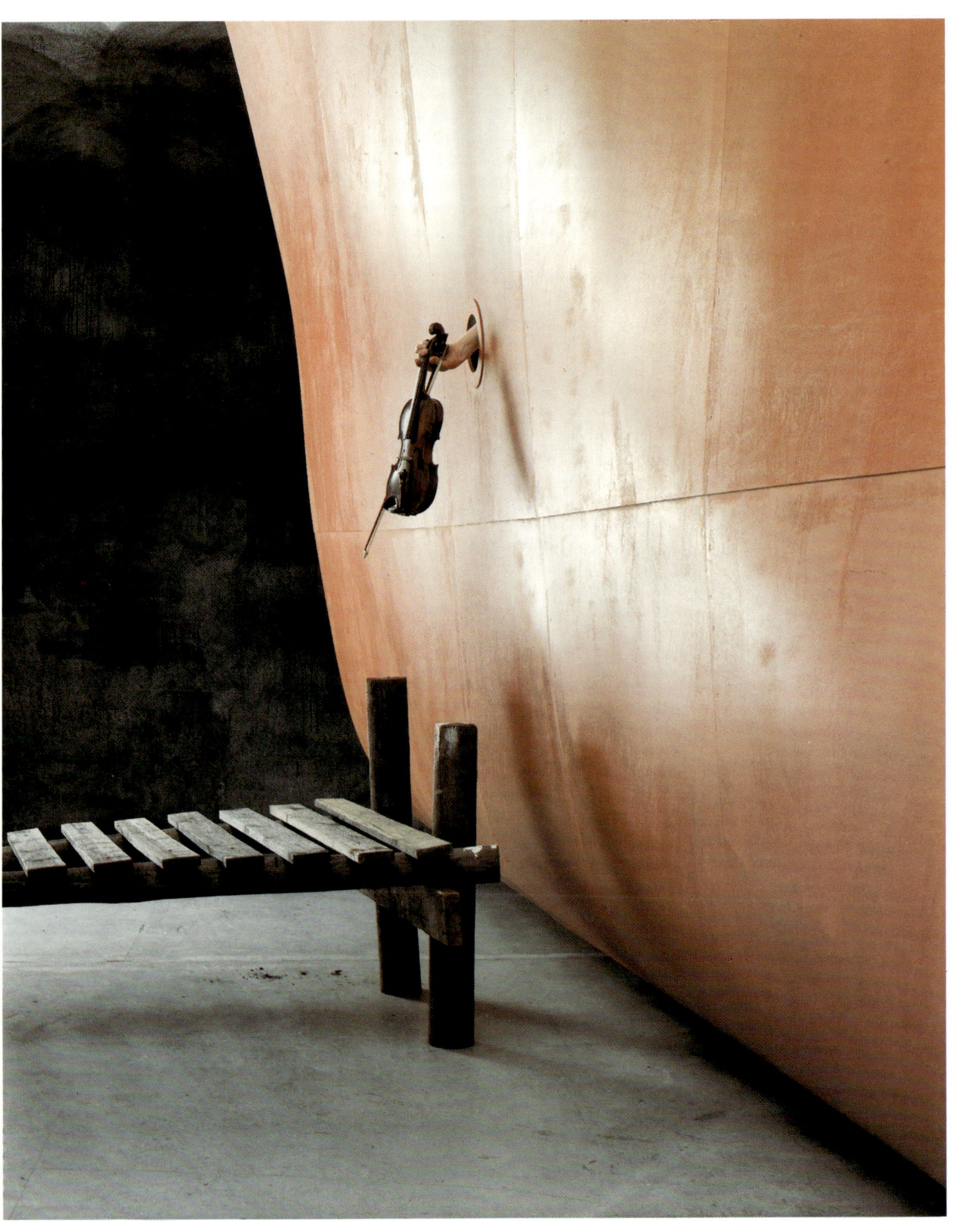

Renounce, 1984
152 × 122 cms
Art Gallery of New South Wales, Sydney

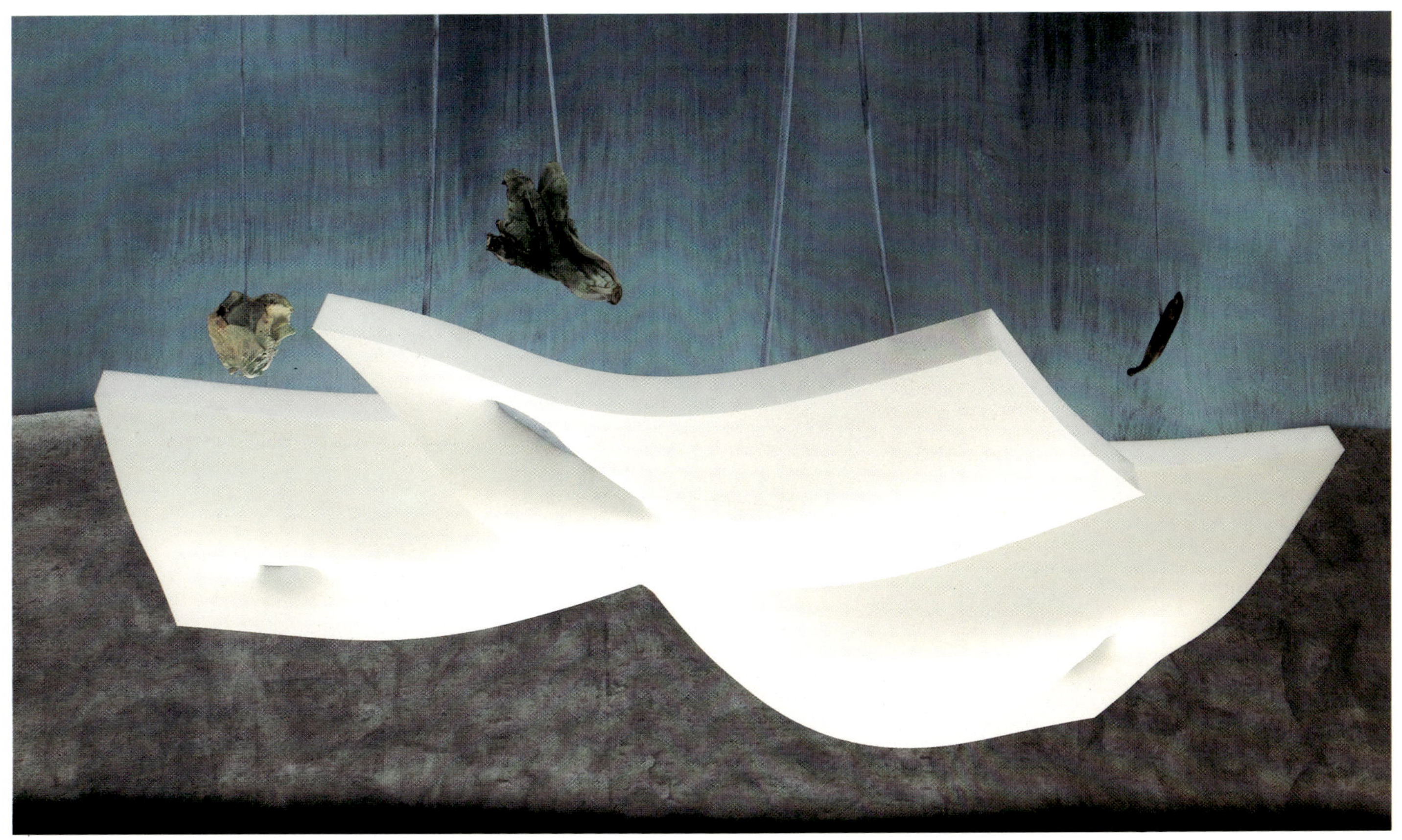

Provisions, 1984
97 × 152 cms
Anthony d'Offay Gallery, London

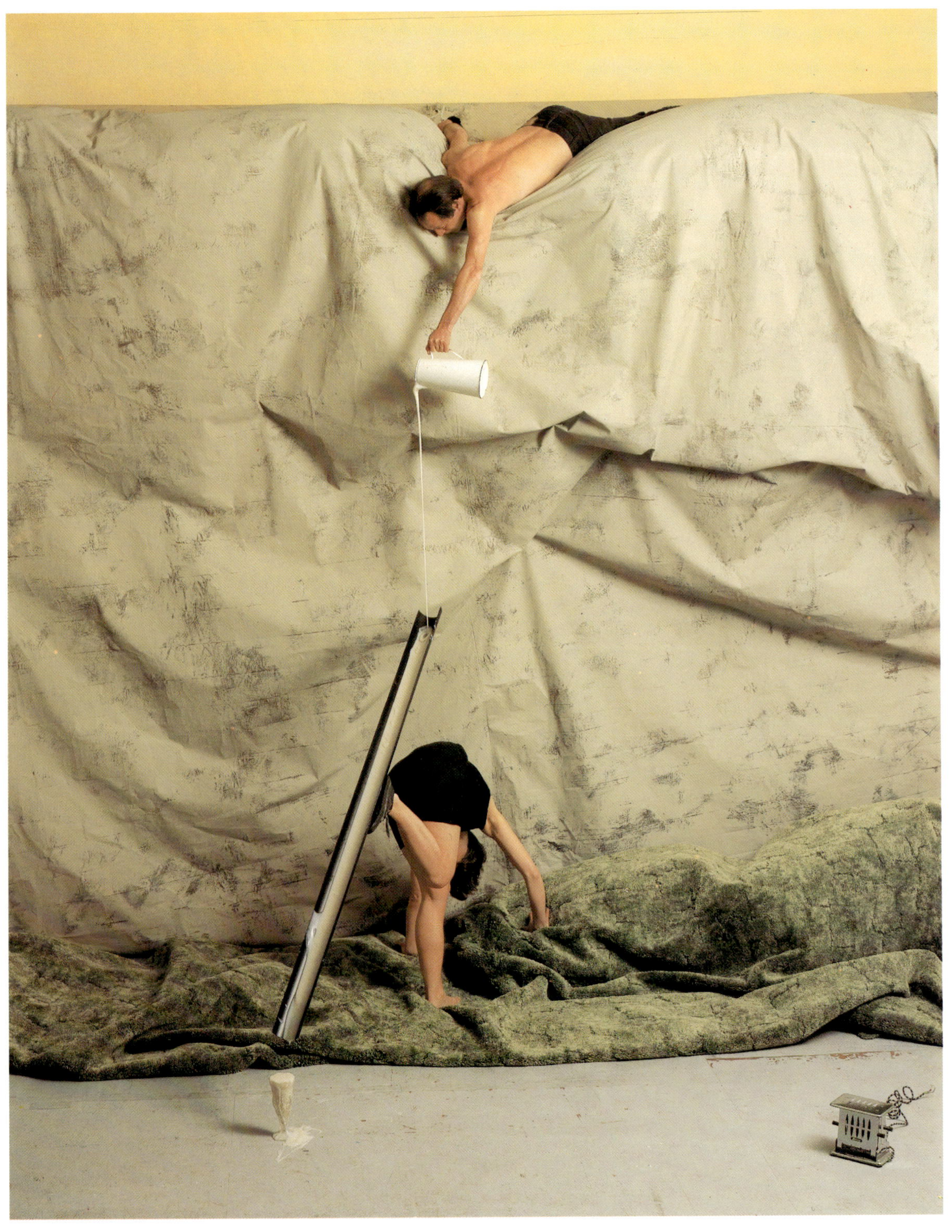

Replenish, 1984
152 × 122 cms
City of Salford Art Galleries

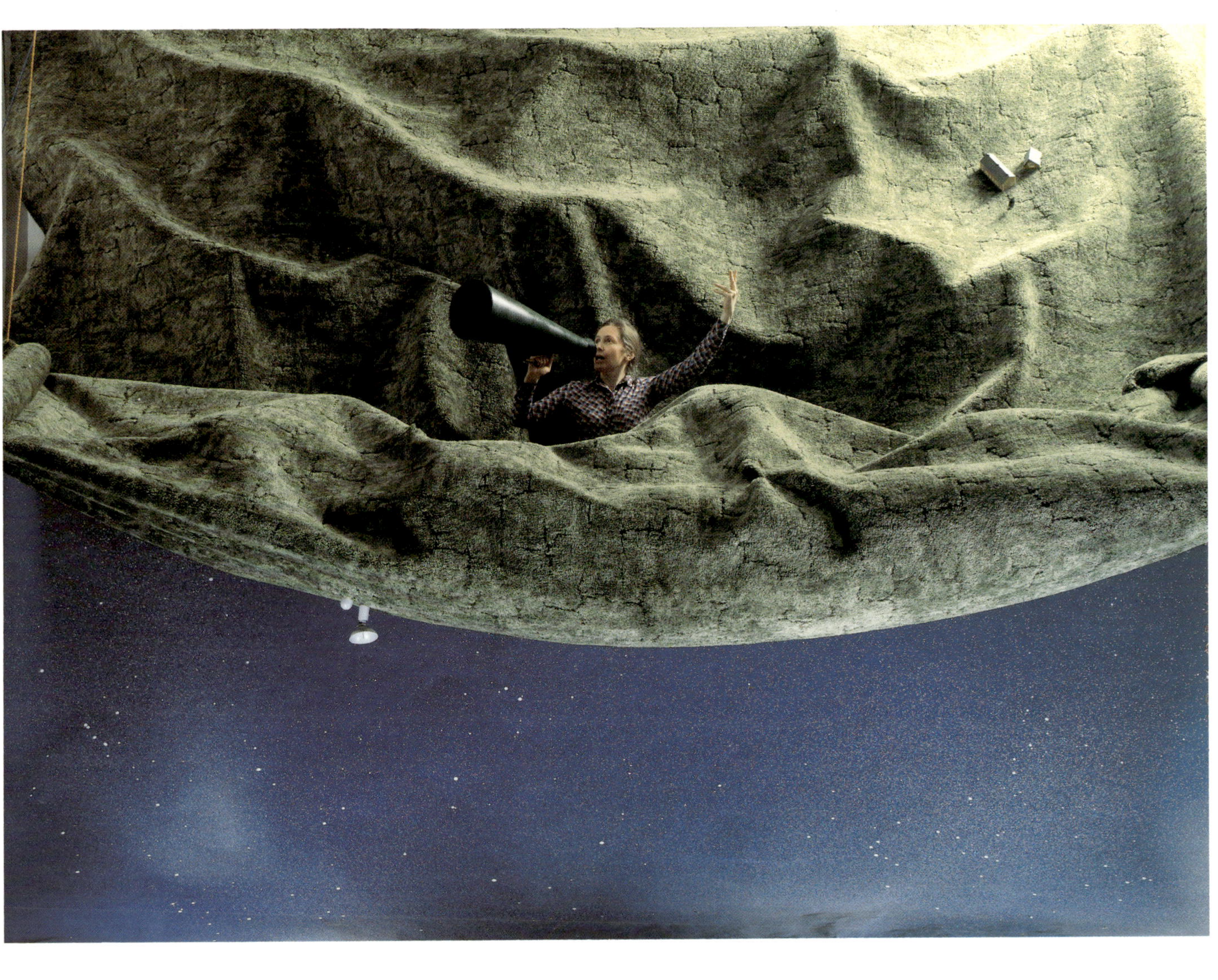

Supplicant, 1984
122 × 152 cms
Marlene Wossman, Cologne

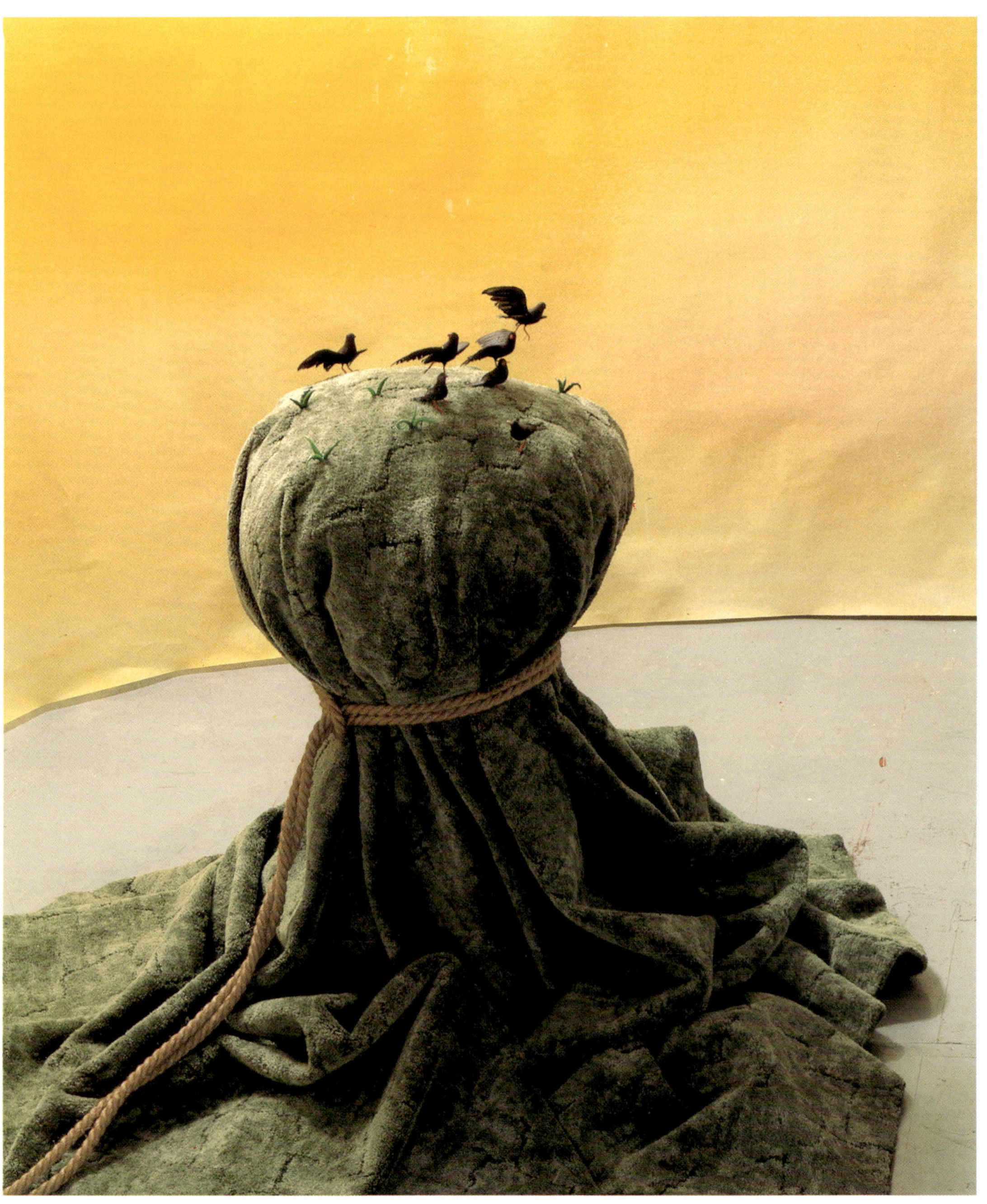

Sphagnum, 1985
152.5 × 122 cms
Sonnabend Gallery, New York

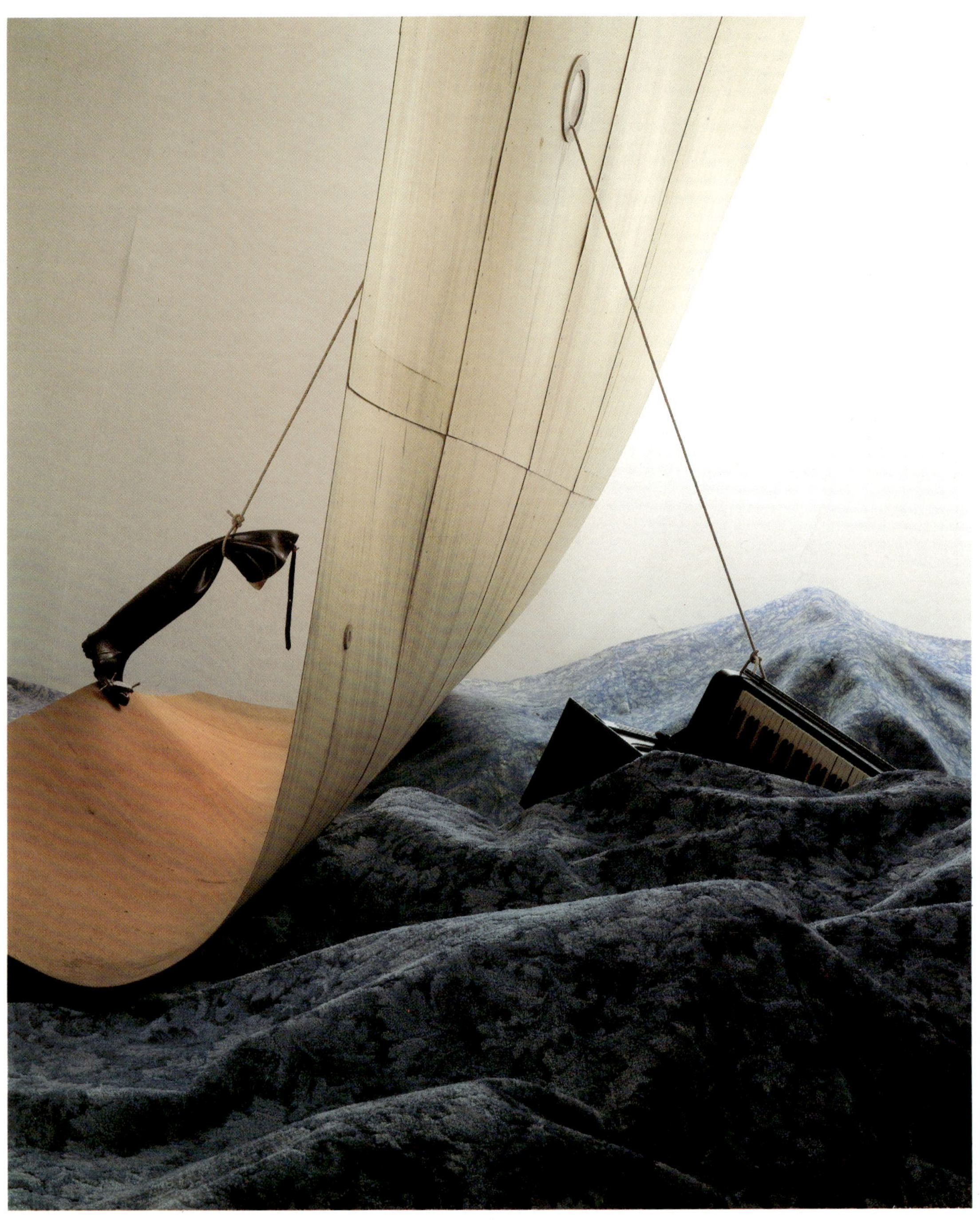

Sargasso, 1985
152 × 122 cms
Wendy and Richard Hokin, Connecticut

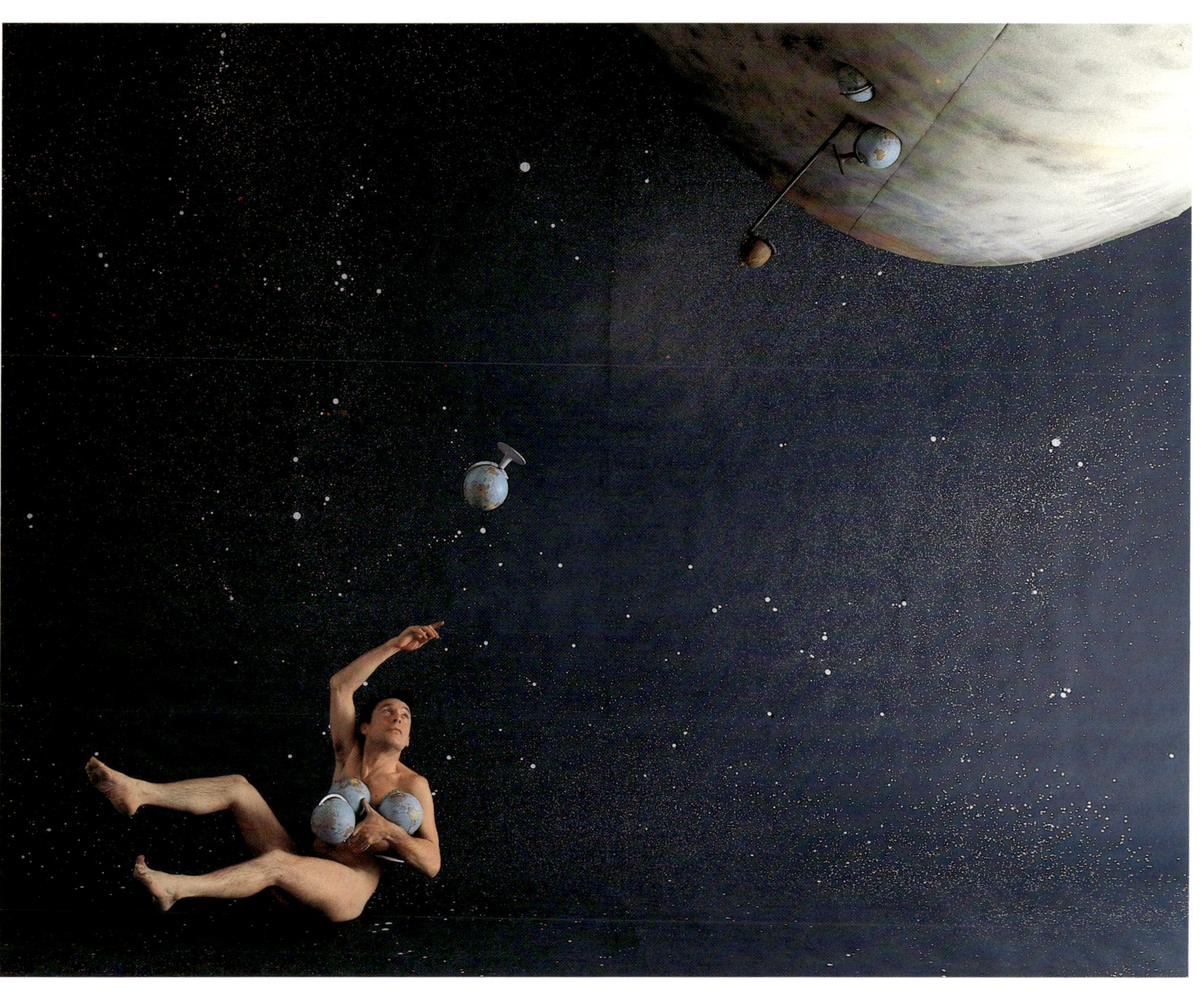

Trophy, 1985
122 × 152 cms
Atlantis Museum, Tenerife

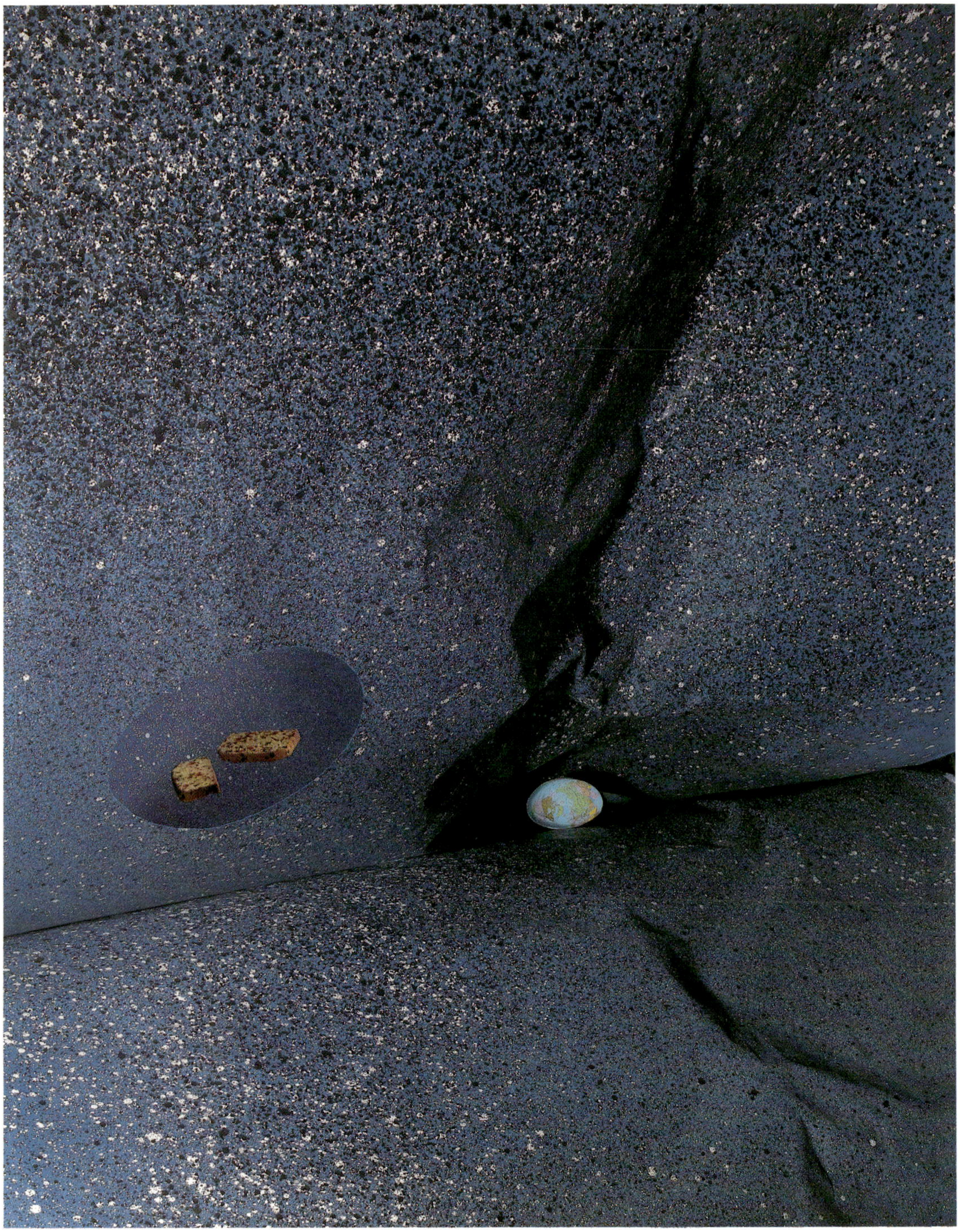

New Rules, 1985
153 × 122 cms
Arts Council of Great Britain

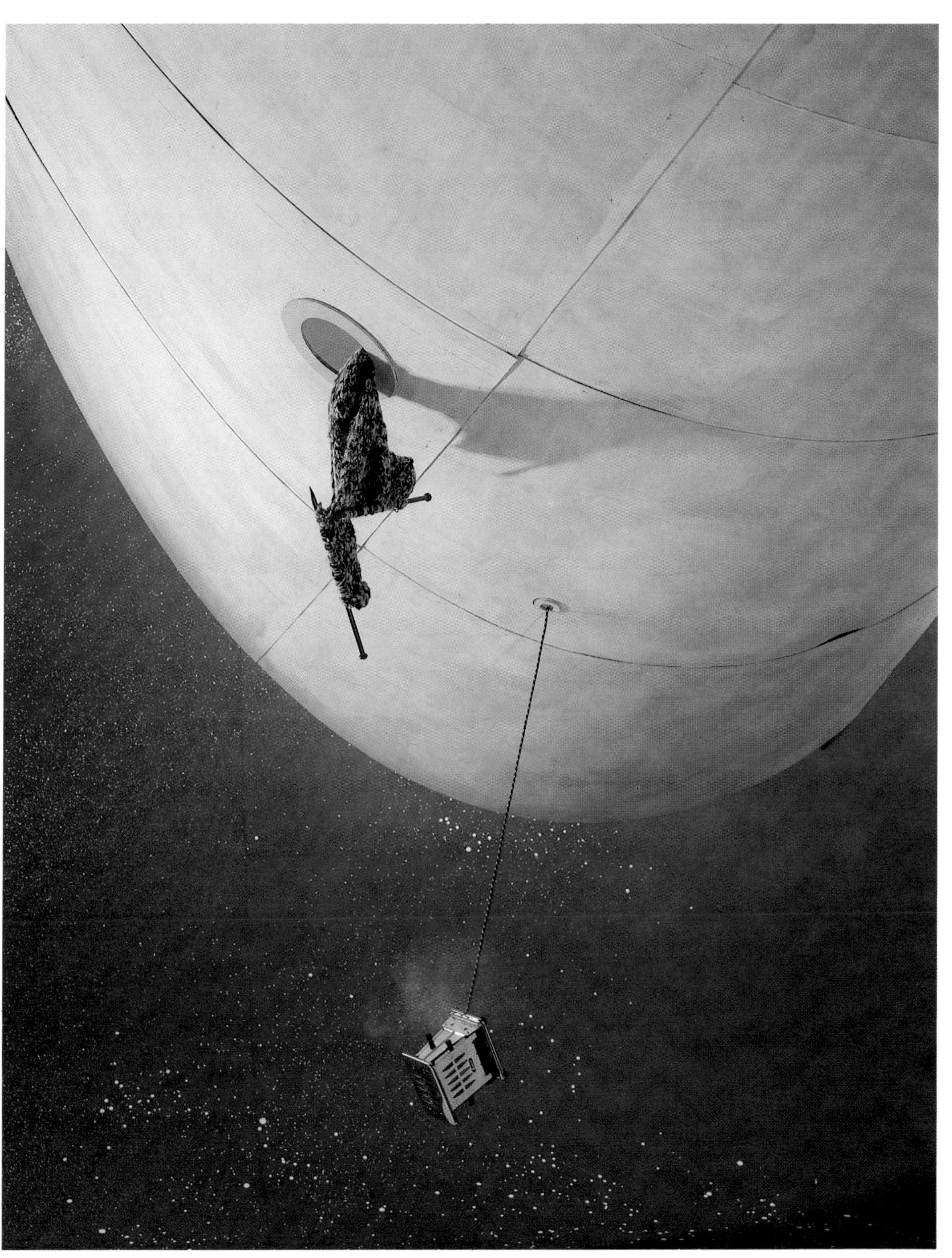

First Principles, 1985
152 × 122 cms
Crousel-Hussenot Gallery, Paris

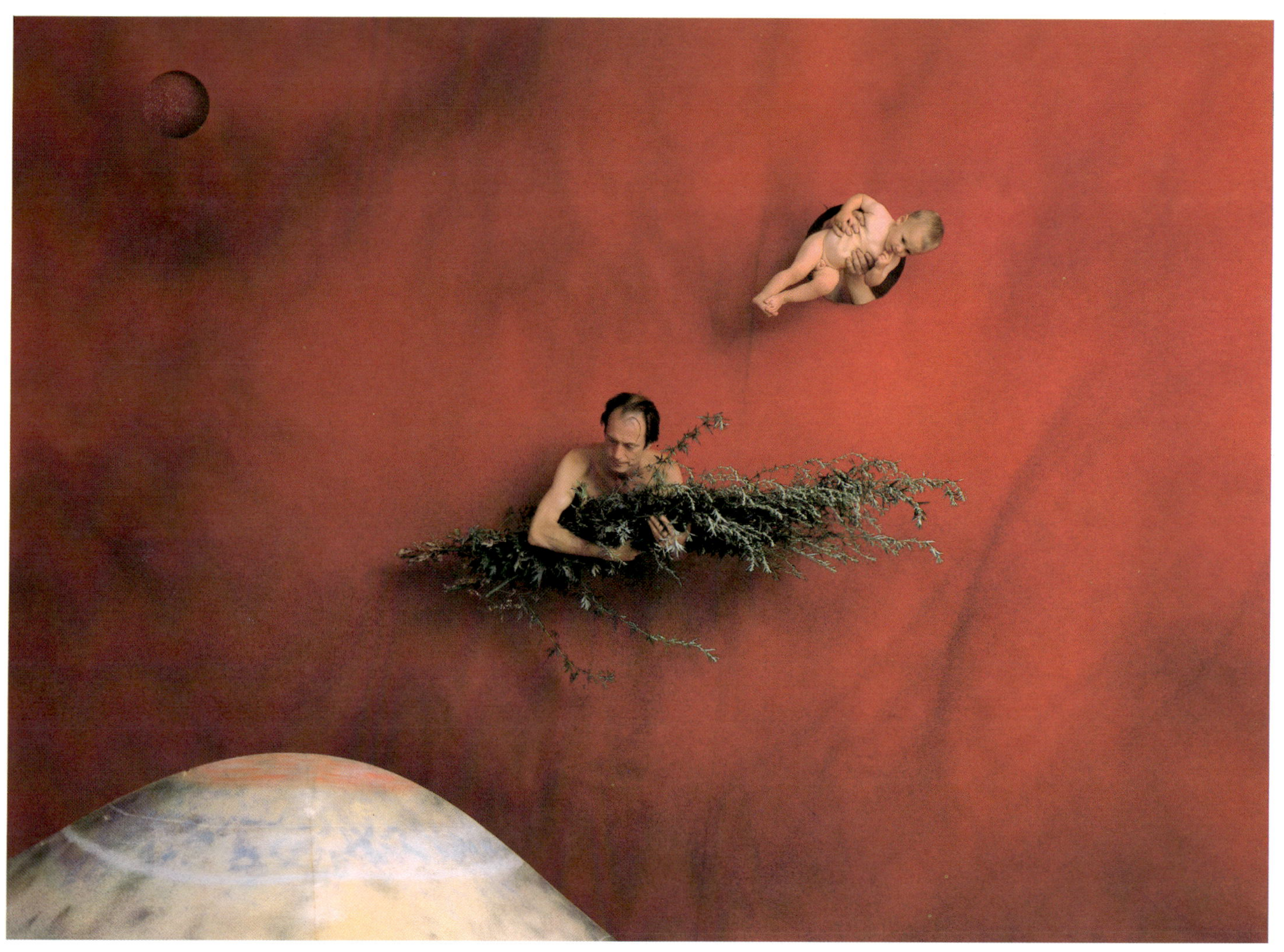

Bedding, 1985
122 × 152.5 cms
Sonnabend Gallery, New York

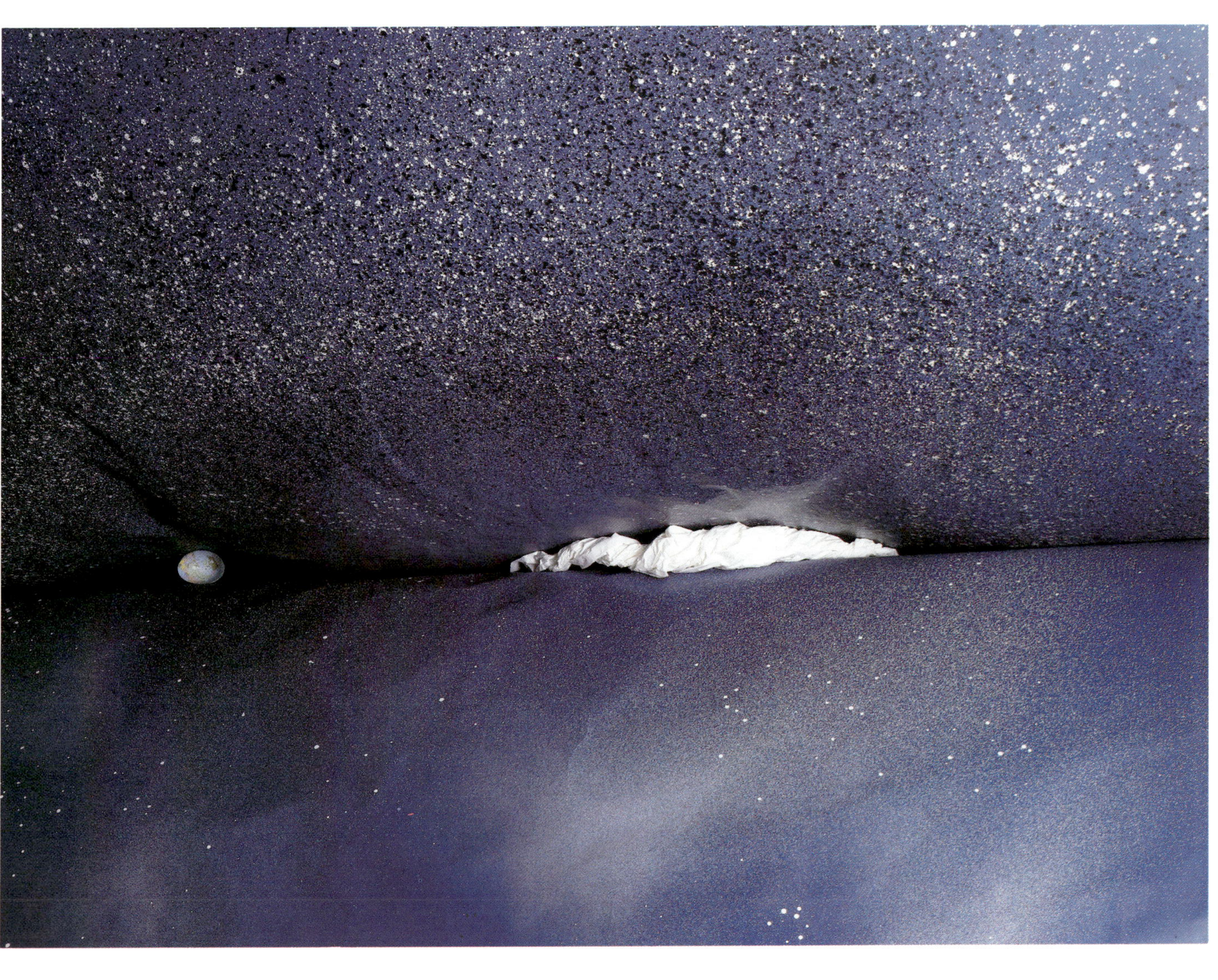

Clenched, 1985
122 × 152.5 cms
Sonnabend Gallery, New York

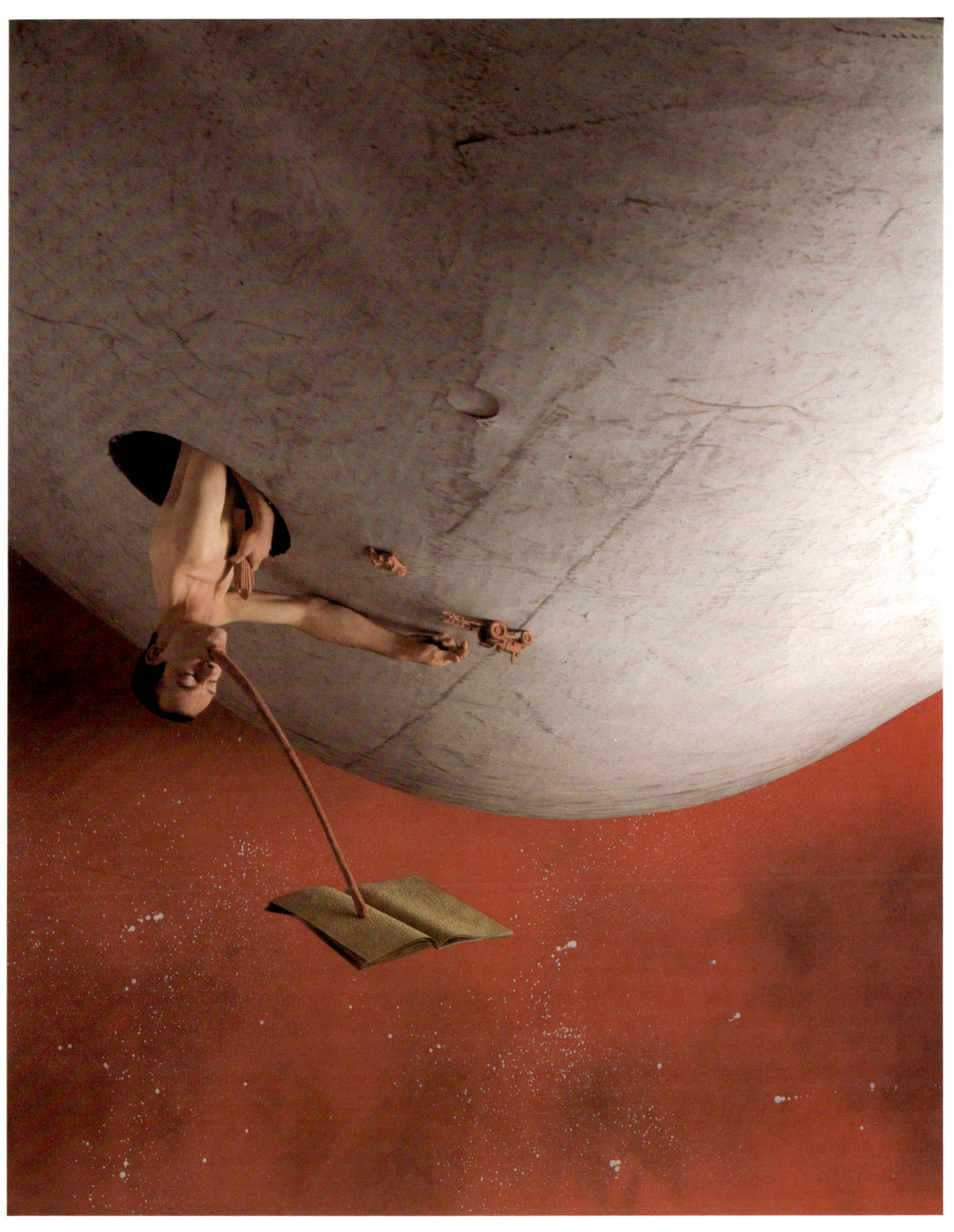

Kibbutz, 1985
152.5 × 122 cms
Sonnabend Gallery, New York

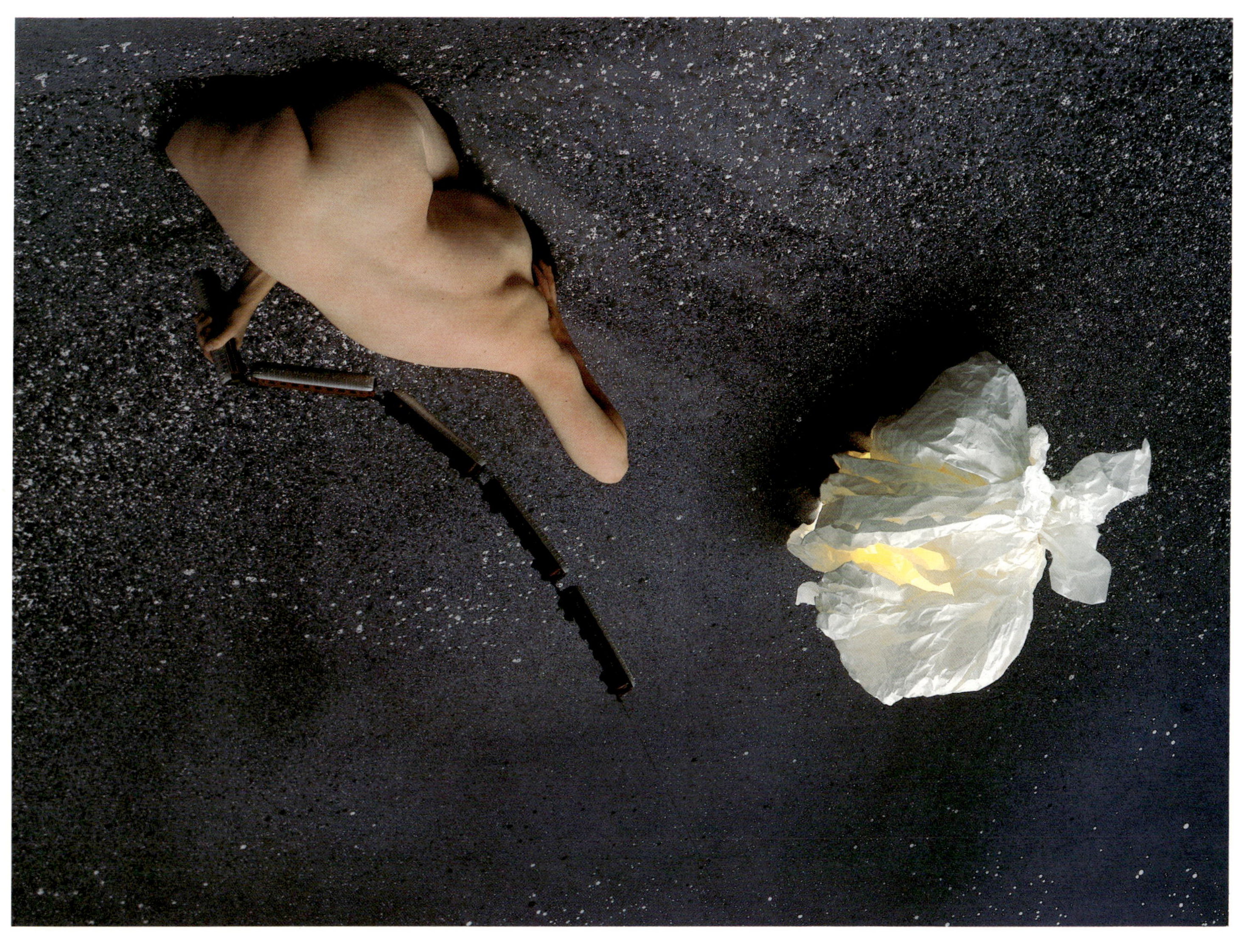

Samurai, 1985
122 × 152 cms
Musée d'art contemporain, Montreal

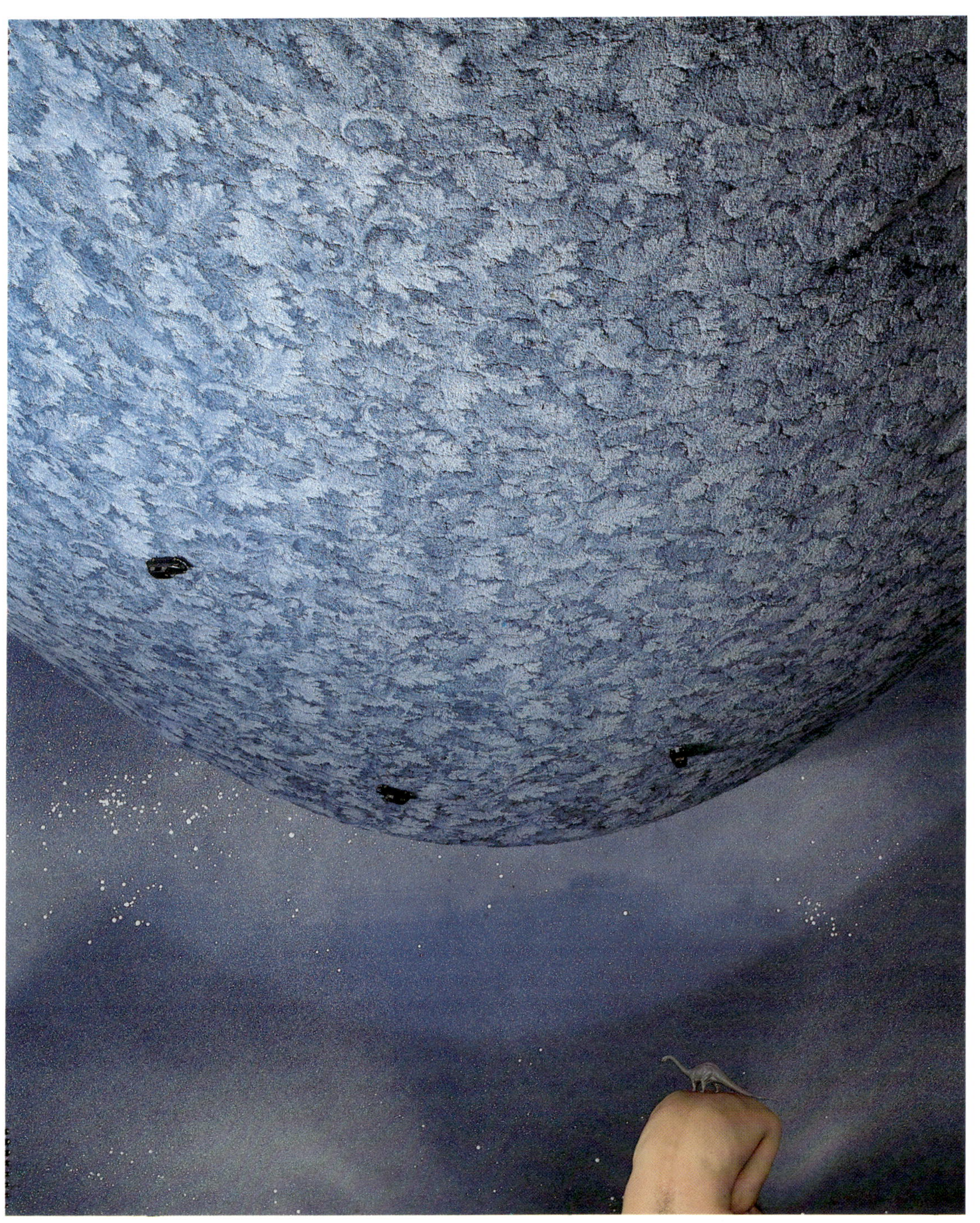

Host, 1985
152 × 122 cms
Fonds National d'Art Contemporain, Paris

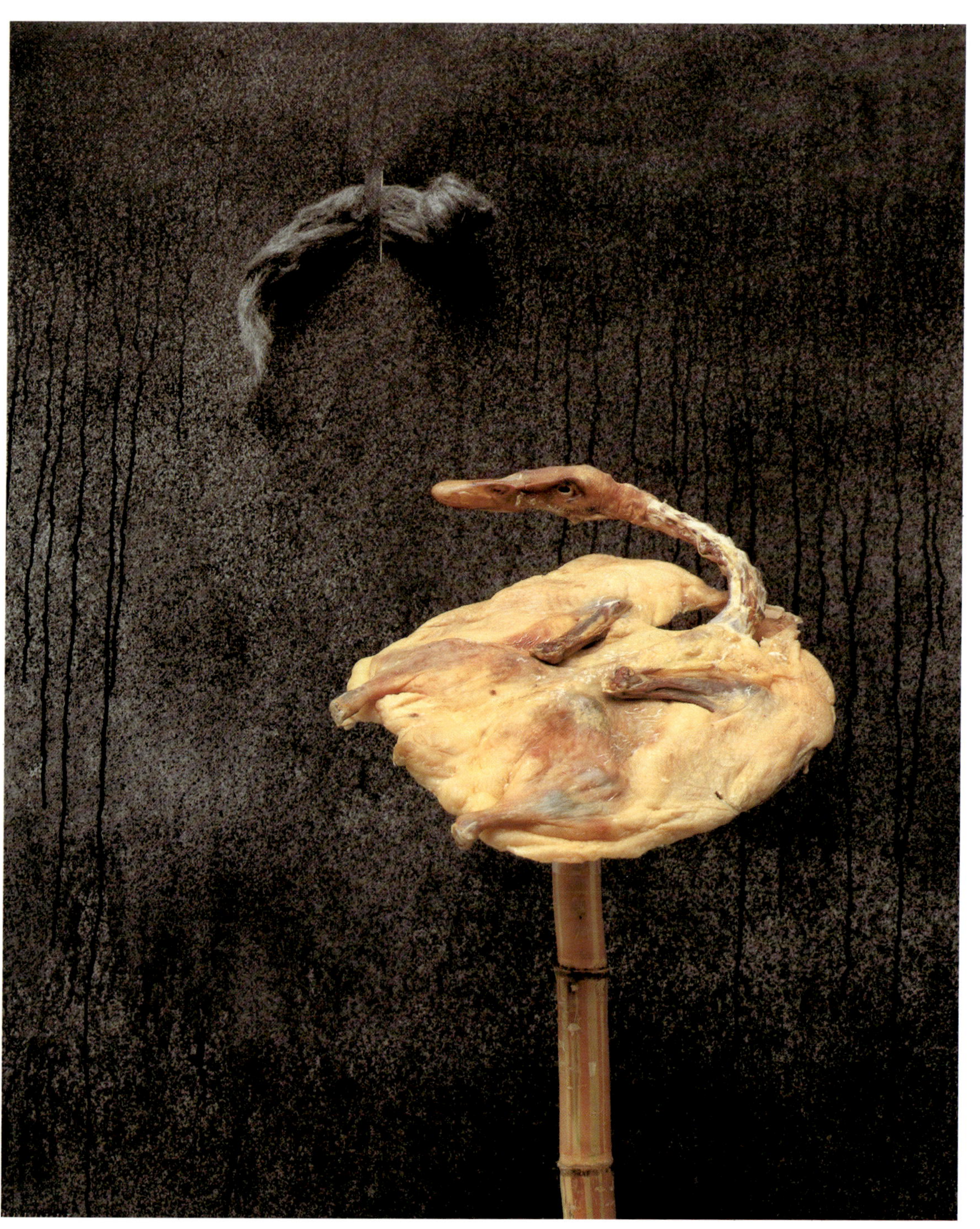

Medallion, 1986
152 × 121 cms
Jean Bernier Gallery, Athens

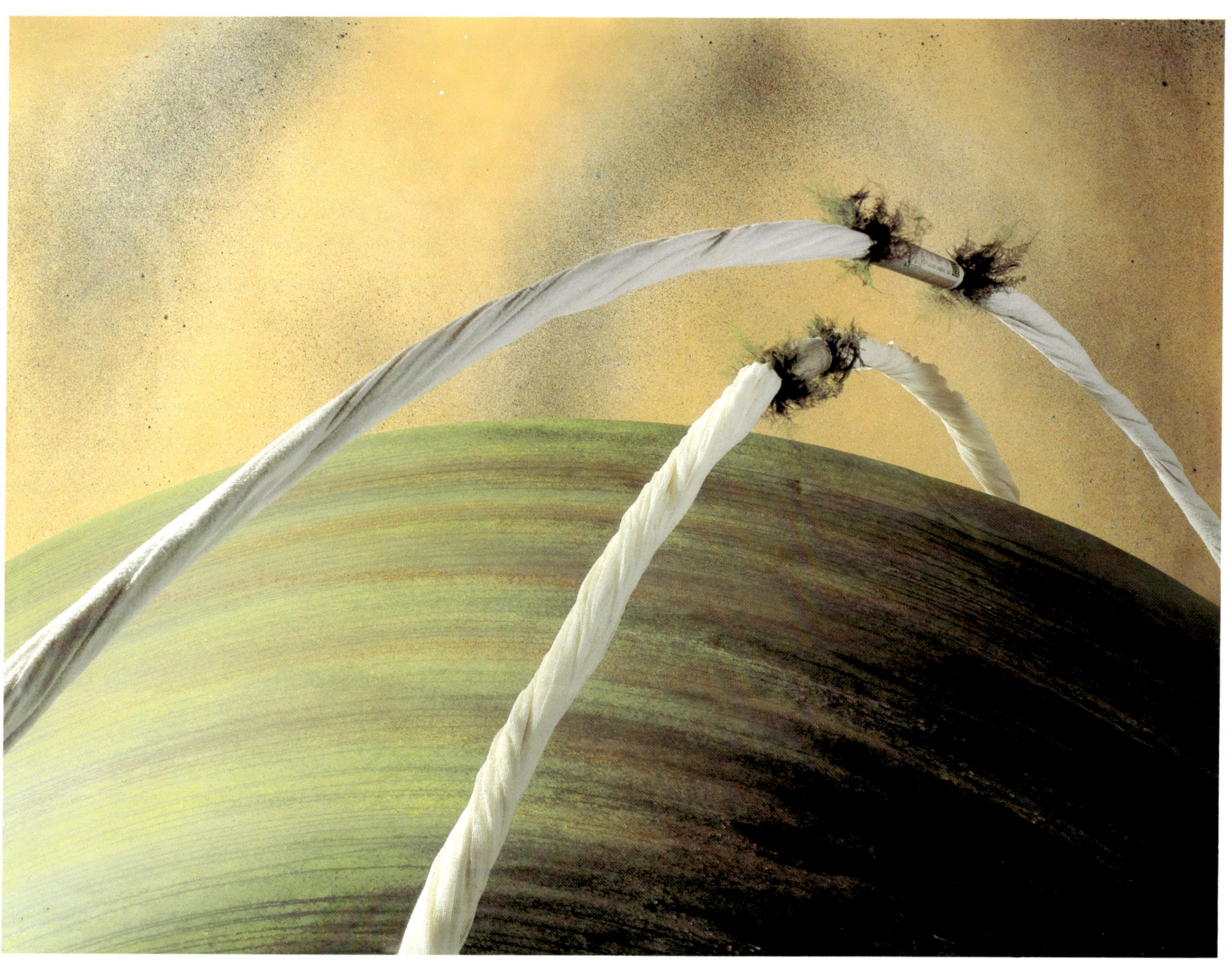

Sprain, 1986
121 × 152 cms
Arrowhead Collection, Athens

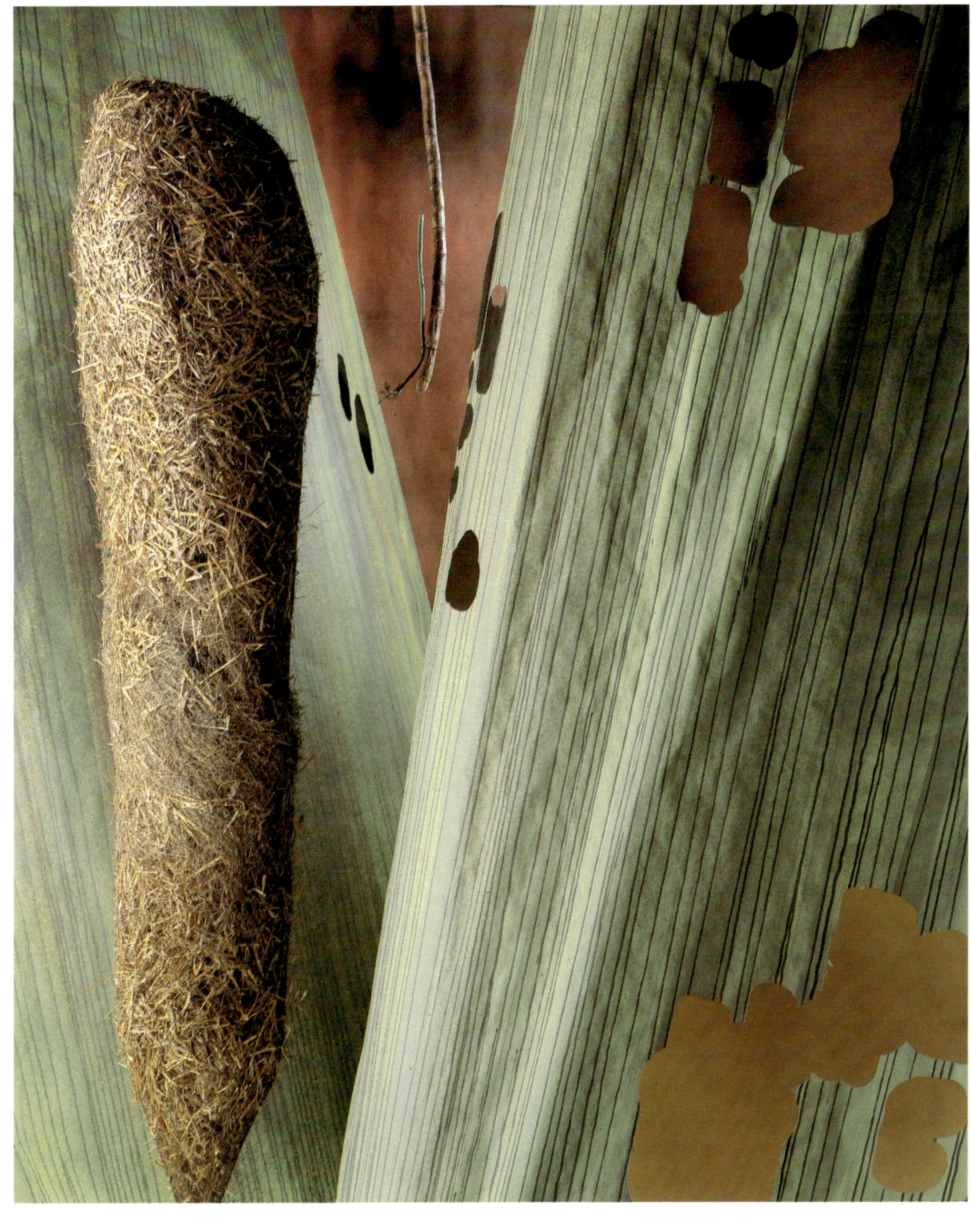

Coppice, 1986
154 × 123 cms
Anthony d'Offay Gallery, London

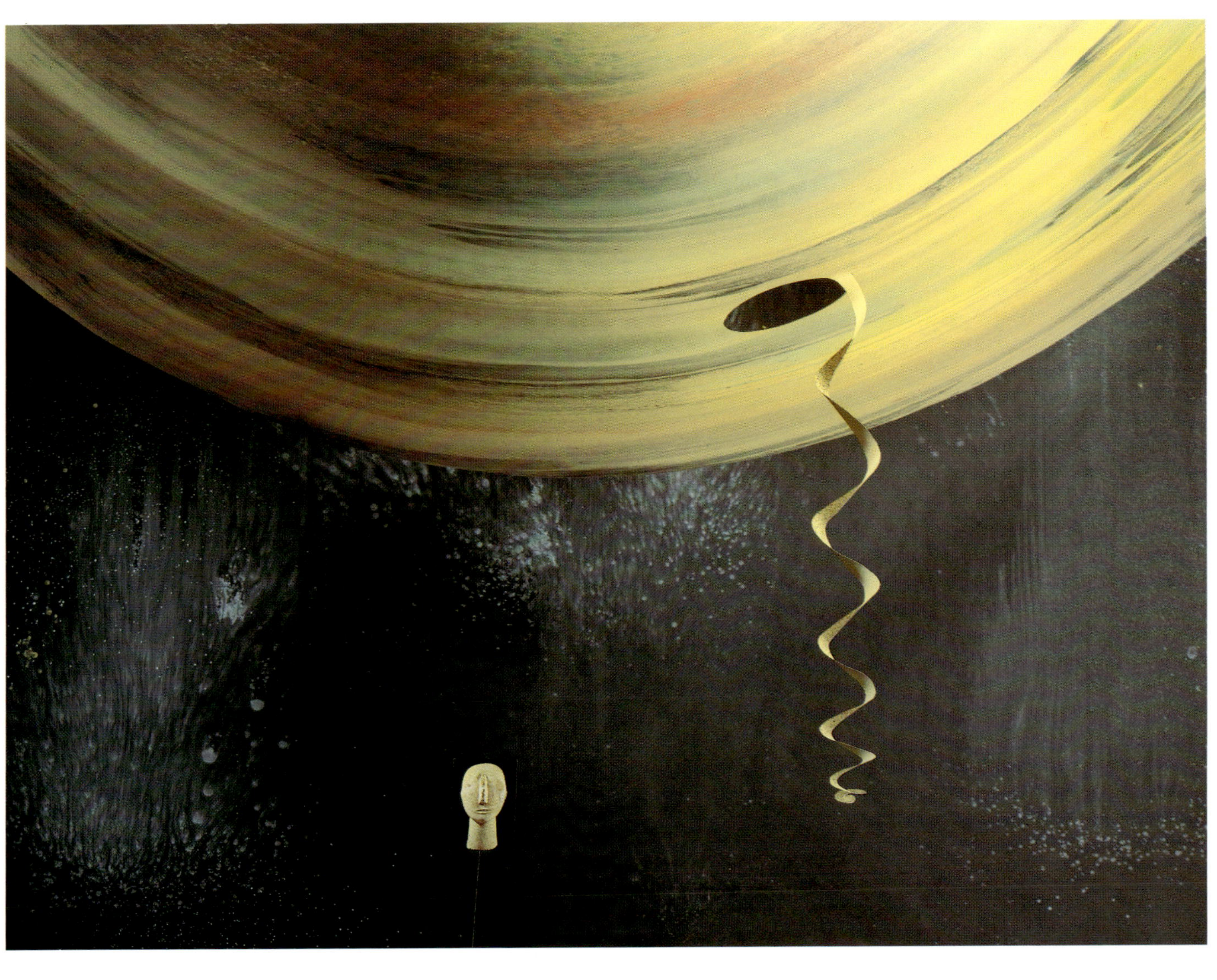

Glorious Morning, 1986
123 × 154 cms
Edwin C. Cohen, New York

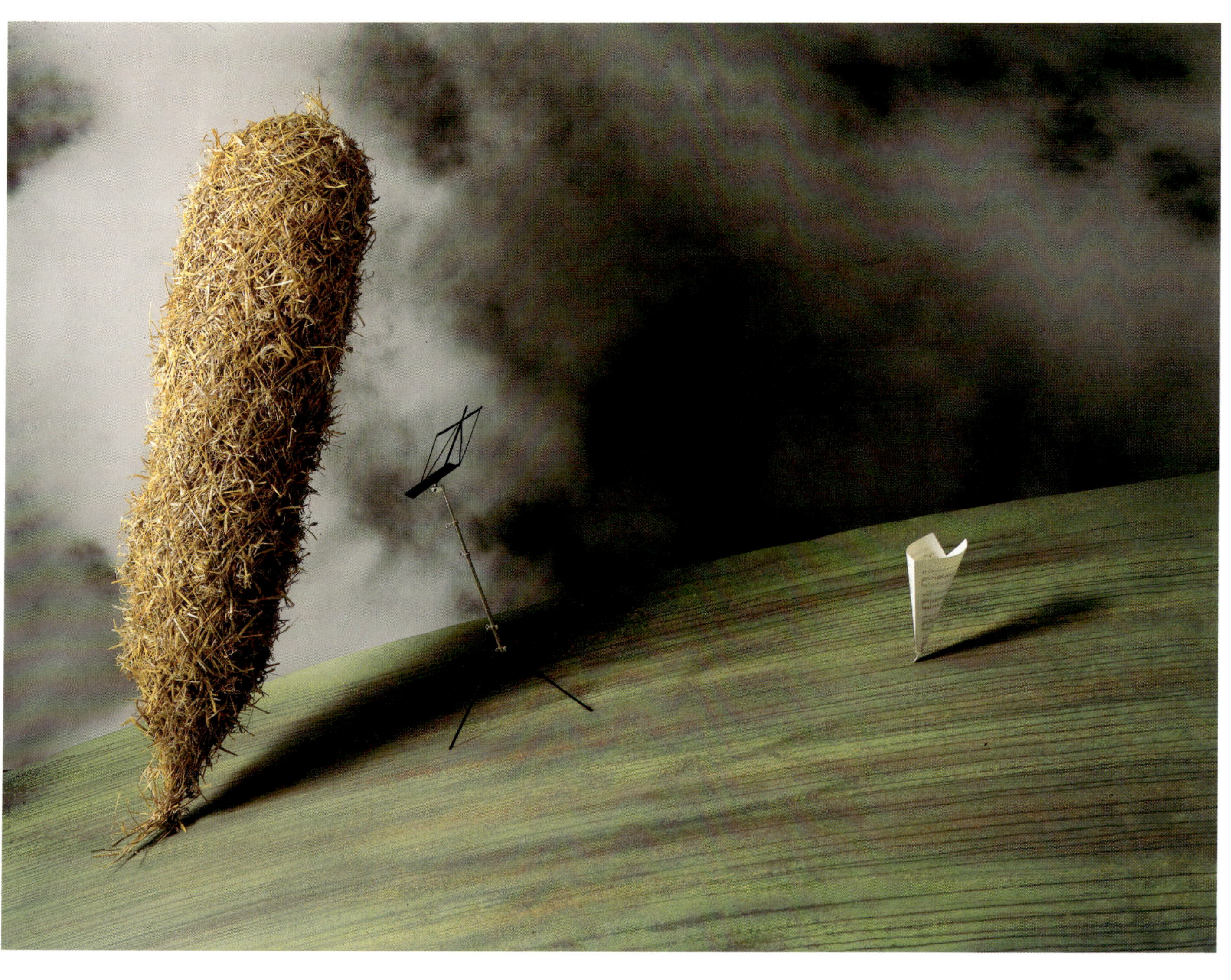

Pupa Rumba Samba, 1986
123 × 154 cms
Williams College Museum of Art, Williamstown, Massachusetts

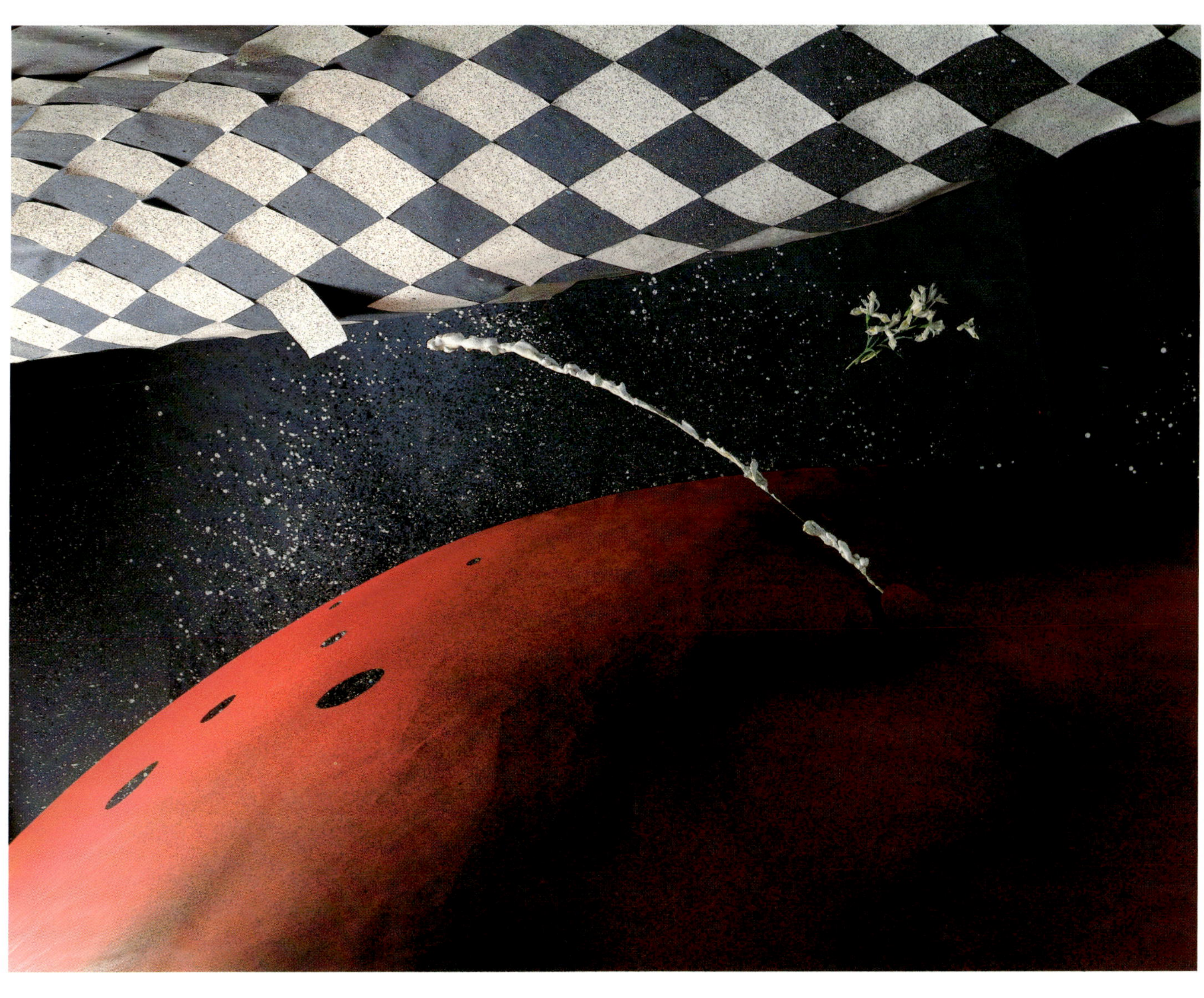

Cupid's String, 1986
123 × 154 cms
Fundacion Cultural Televisa, Mexico

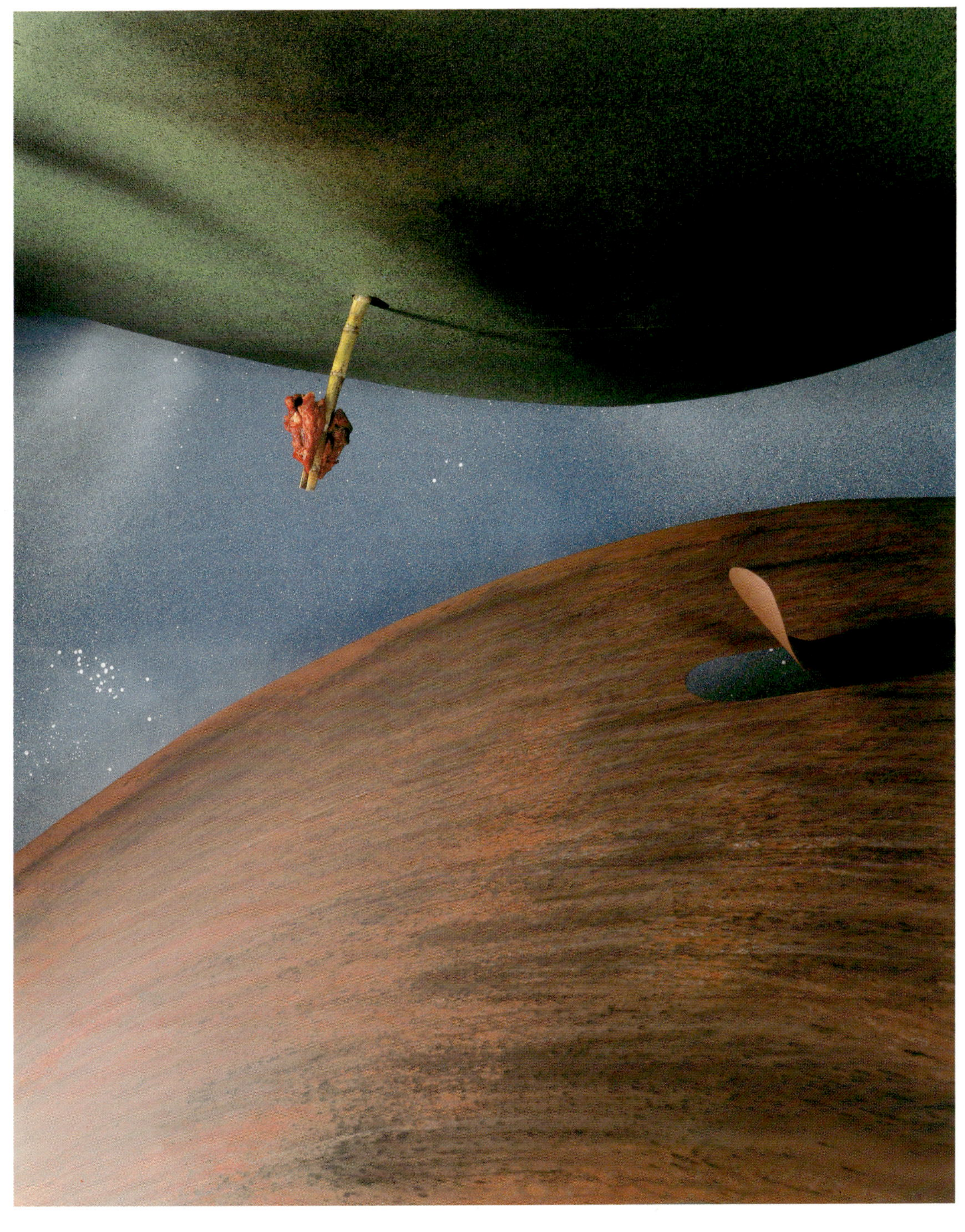

Recruit, 1986
152 × 122 cms
Private collection, Athens

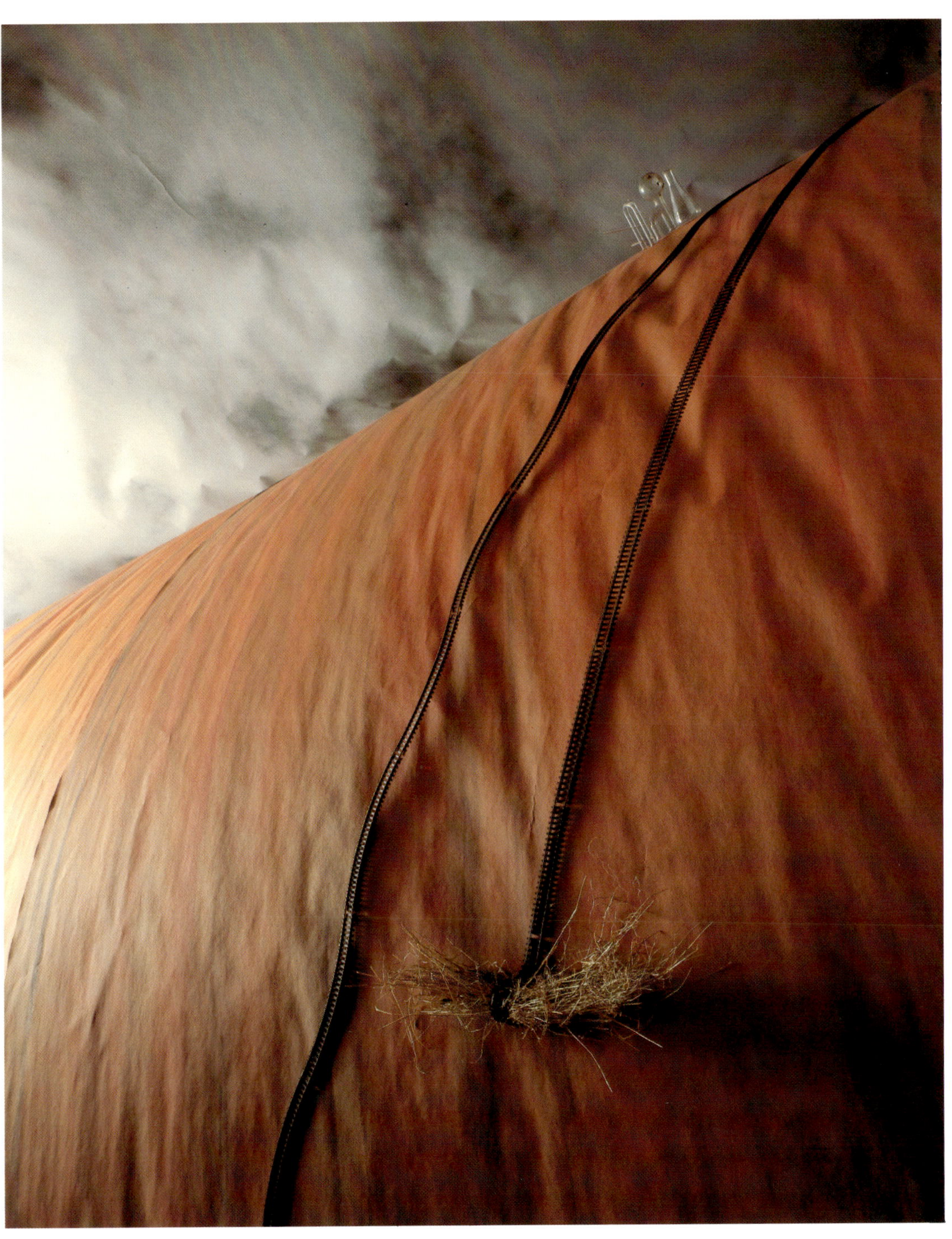

Enzyme, 1986
154 × 123 cms
Karl Bornstein Gallery, Santa Monica

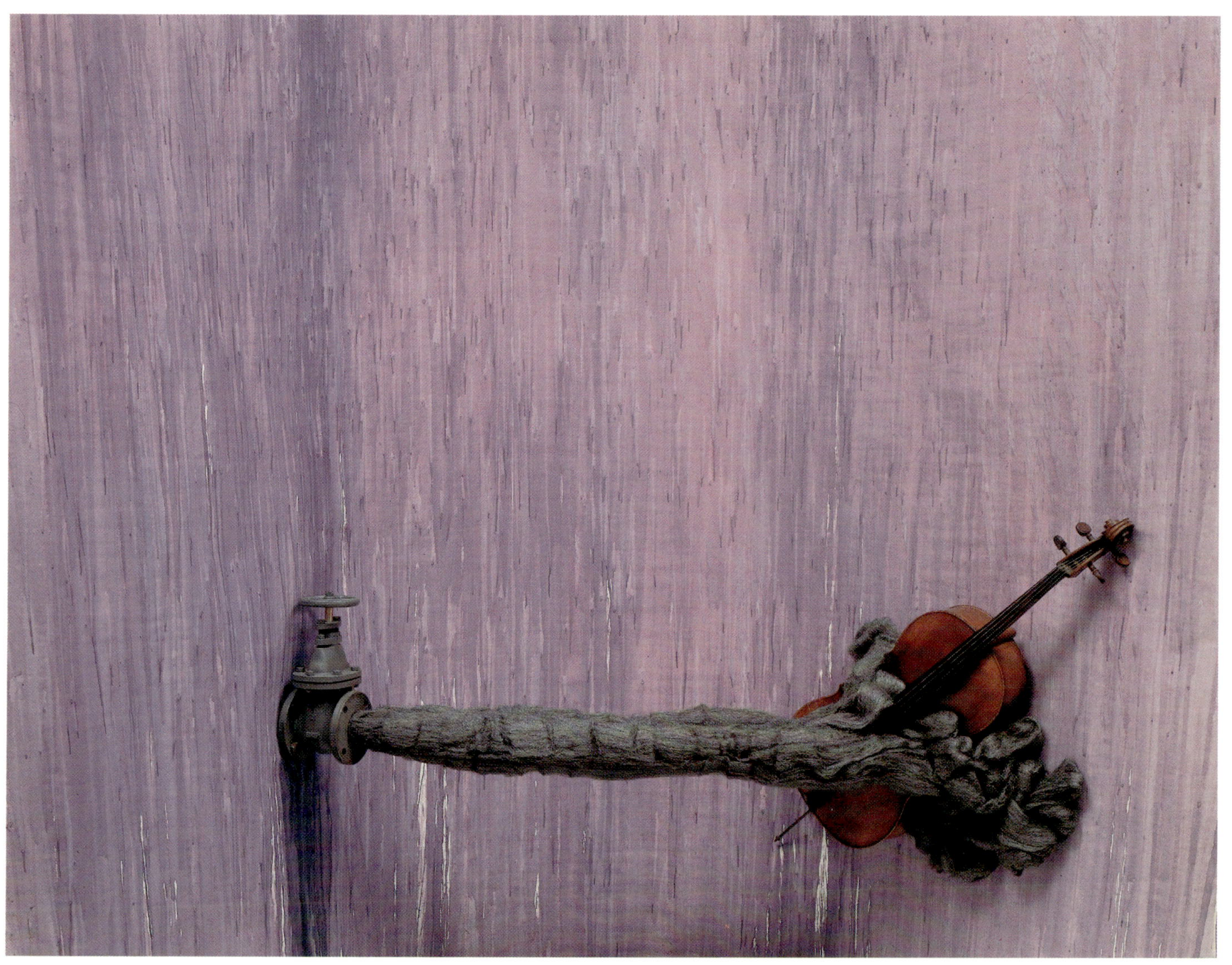

Coda, 1987
123 × 154 cms
Anthony d'Offay Gallery, London

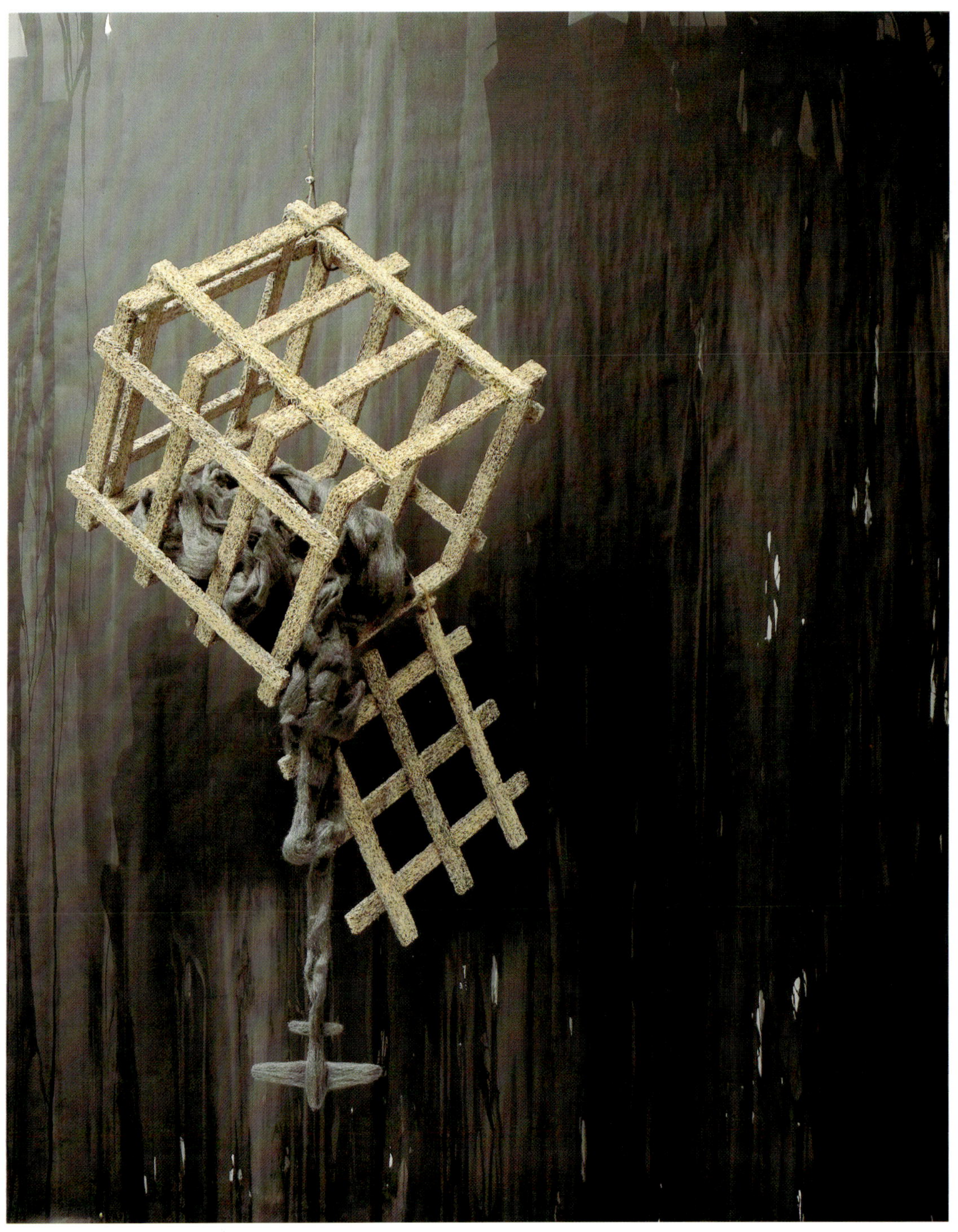

Untitled, 1987
154 × 123 cms
Anthony d'Offay Gallery, London

Biography & Bibliography

1947   Born in Christchurch, New Zealand
1968-71 Studied at Ilam School of Art
1972-75 Studied at Royal College of Art, London
        Lives and works in London

Selected One-Man Exhibitions

1976   Robert Self Gallery, London
1977   Graves Art Gallery, Sheffield
        Robert Self Gallery, Newcastle
        Graeme Murray Gallery, Edinburgh
1978   Gray Art Gallery and Museum, Hartlepool
        Konrad Fischer Gallery, Düsseldorf
        Jean and Karen Bernier Gallery, Athens
        Arnolfini Gallery, Bristol (travelled to Chapter
        Art Centre, Cardiff)
        Whitechapel Art Gallery, London
1979   New 57 Gallery, Edinburgh
        Sonnabend Gallery, New York

        Galerie Sonnabend, Paris
1980   Galerie 't Venster, Rotterdam
        Museum Haus Lange, Krefeld
1981   Galerie Loyse Oppenheim, Geneva
        Anthony d'Offay Gallery, London
        John Hansard Gallery, Southampton
        Auckland City Art Gallery, Auckland,
        New Zealand (travelled to other galleries in
        New Zealand including the National Gallery,
        Wellington)
        Sonnabend Gallery, New York
1982   Badischer Kunstverein, Karlsruhe (travelled to
        Westfälischer Kunstverein, Münster)
        Jean and Karen Bernier Gallery, Athens
1983   Centre Georges Pompidou, Paris
        Galerie Crousel-Hussenot, Paris
        Stedelijk Van Abbemuseum, Eindhoven
        (travelled to Kunsthalle, Bern; Le Nouveau
        Musée, Lyon; Leeds City Art Gallery; Musée
        Municipale, La Roche-sur-Yon)
1984   Anthony d'Offay Gallery, London

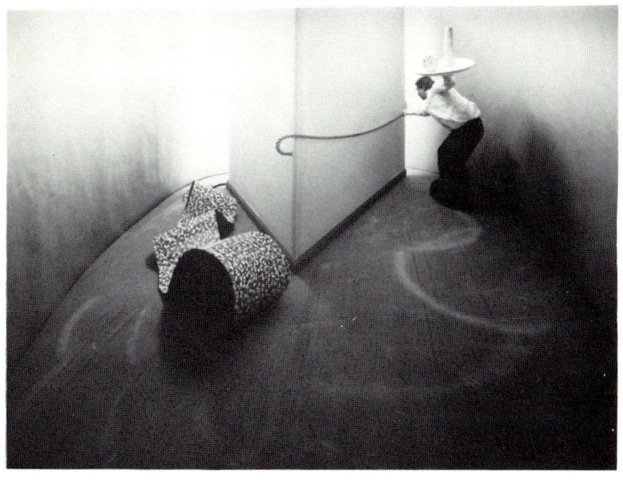

Untitled (waiter), 1981,
Unique colour photograph, 63.5 × 89.5 cms,
Anthony d'Offay Gallery, London

1985   University of Northern Illinois, Chicago
(travelled to University of Massachusetts,
Amherst; University of Tenessee, Knoxville;
University Art Museum, California State
University, Long Beach)
Sonnabend Gallery, New York
Chapter Art Centre, Cardiff
1986   Adelaide Festival, Adelaide (travelled to
Australian Centre for Contemporary Art,
Melbourne; Centre for the Arts, University of
Tasmania; Power Gallery of Contemporary Art,
University of Sydney)
Sue Crockford Gallery, Auckland
Jean Bernier Gallery, Athens

Selected Group Exhibitions

1975   Robert Self Gallery, London
1976   *Pan Pacific Biennale* Auckland, New Zealand
1977   *Time, Words and the Camera,* Kunstlerhaus,
Graz (travelled to Galerie im Taxispalais,
Innsbruck; Kunstlerhaus, Vienna; Museum
Bochum, Bochum)
1979   *Europa 79,* Stuttgart
With a Certain Smile, InK, Zürich
1980   *Artist and Camera,* Arts Council touring
exhibition (Sunderland Art Centre; Bluecoat
Gallery, Open Eye Gallery and School of

Architecture, Liverpool; Mostyn Art Gallery,
Llandudno; Southampton Art Gallery and John
Hansard Gallery; Arnolfini Gallery, Bristol;
Institute of Contemporary Arts, London)
About 70 Photographs, Arts Council touring
exhibition
Photography and the Medium, British Council
touring exhibition (travelled to Norway,
Poland, Yugoslavia, The Netherlands, Denmark
and Spain)
Sonnabend Gallery, New York
Lisson Gallery, London
Photographic Contrivances, University of
California, Santa Barbara
1981   *Fabricated to be Photographed,* Wright State
University, Dayton, Ohio
P.S.1, New York
New Works of Contemporary Art and Music,
Fruitmarket Gallery, Edinburgh
New Directions, Sidney Janis Gallery, New York

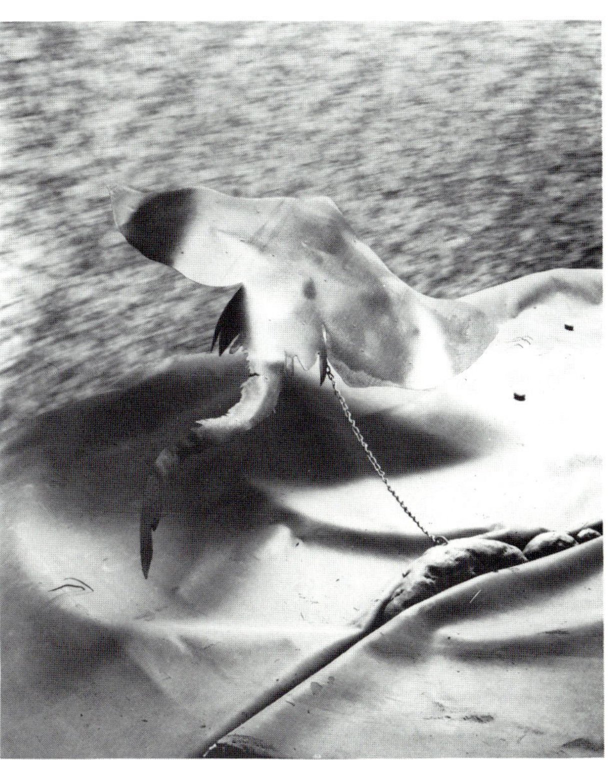

Untitled (tethered ray), 1981,
Unique colour photograph, 97 × 71.5 cms,
Musée National d'Art Moderne, Centre Georges Pompidou, Paris

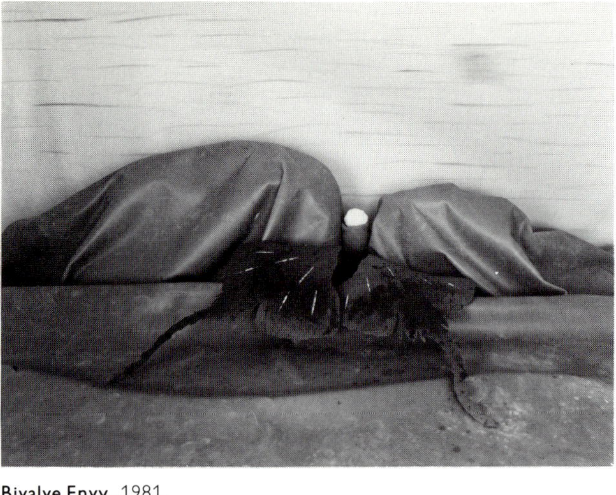

Bivalve Envy, 1981,
Unique colour photograph, 67 × 96.5 cms,
Musée National d'Art Moderne, Centre Georges Pompidou, Paris

The New Colour, Everson Museum of Art,
Syracuse, New York
Art and the Sea, Third Eye Centre, Glasgow
(travelled to Mappin Art Gallery, Sheffield;
Stoke City Art Gallery; DLI Museum and Arts
Centre, Durham; Cartwright Hall, Bradford)
Sonnabend Gallery, New York
Anthony d'Offay Gallery, London
Galerie Chantal Crousel, Paris
Erweiterte Fotografie, Neue Secession, Vienna
Das Porträt in der Fotografie, Rheinisches
Landesmuseum, Bonn

1982   *Fourth Biennale of Sydney*, Sydney, Australia
Staged Photo Events, Lijnbaan Centrum,
Rotterdam
Documenta 7, Kassel

1983   *The Sculpture Show*, Hayward Gallery, London
Images Fabriquées, Centre Georges Pompidou,
Paris

1984   *Histoires de Sculpture*, Château des Ducs
d'Epernon, Cadillac, Gironde
Anxious Interiors, Laguna Beach Museum of Art,
California
The British Art Show, Arts Council touring
exhibition (travelled to City of Birmingham
Museum and Art Gallery and Ikon Gallery;
Royal Scottish Academy, Edinburgh; Mappin Art
Gallery Sheffield; Southampton Art Gallery)

1985   *L'Indifférent*, John Hansard Gallery,
Southampton
Paris Biennale, Grande Halle de la Villette, Paris
Alles und noch viel Mehr, Kunsthalle, Bern
The Irresistible Object: Still Life 1600-1985,
Leeds City Art Gallery
Atelier Polaroid, Centre Georges Pompidou,
Paris

1986   *Forty Years of Modern Art 1945-1985*, Tate
Gallery, London
Sculpture: 9 Artists from England, Louisiana
Museum, Humlebaek, Denmark
The Real Big Picture, Queens Museum,
New York
Collection Souvenir, Le Nouveau Musée, Lyon
Aperto, Venice Biennale
Prospect 86, Frankfurter Kunstverein and Schirn
Kunsthalle, Frankfurt
Contrariwise: Surrealism and Britain 1930-1986,
Glynn Vivian Art Gallery, Swansea (travelled to
Victoria Art Gallery, Bath; Polytechnic Gallery,
Newcastle; Mostyn Art Gallery, Llandudno)

1987   *'Blow Up' Zeitgeschichte*, Württembergischer
Kunstverein, Stuttgart (travels to Haus am
Waldsee, Berlin; Kunstverein, Hamburg;
Frankfurter Kunstverein; Kunstmuseum,
Luzern; Rheinisches Landesmuseum, Bonn)
Contemporary British Photography, British
Council touring exhibition (travels to Belgium,
Luxembourg and Italy)

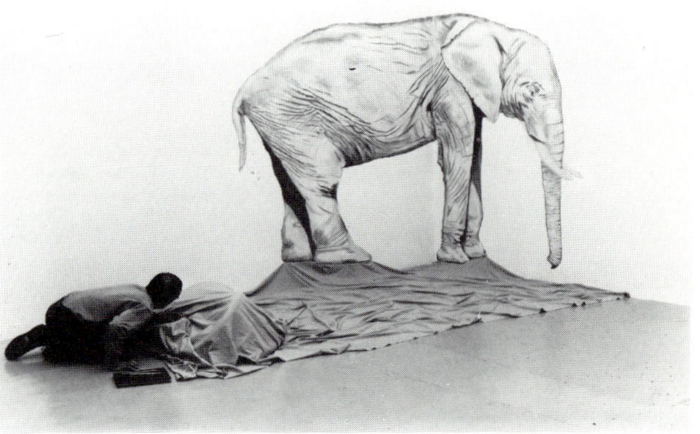

Survey, 1982,
Unique colour photograph, 76 × 102 cms,
Kunsthaus, Zürich

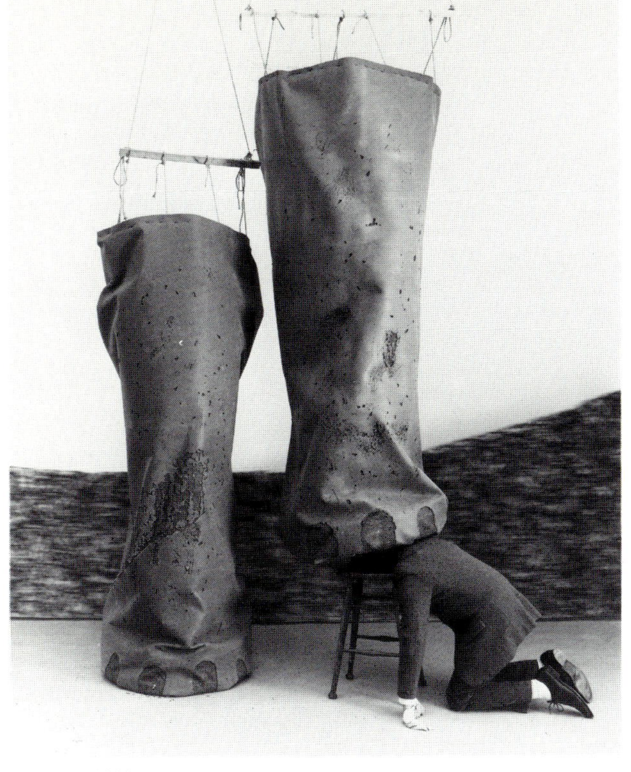

Untitled, 1982,
Unique colour photograph, 122 × 92 cms,
Boyd Webb

Selected Bibliography

Stuart Morgan, *Tableaux,* catalogue, Robert Self Gallery, London, 1978
Nicholas Serota, 'Contrary Illuminations', *Boyd Webb,* catalogue, Whitechapel Art Gallery, London, 1978
Marianne Stockebrand, *Boyd Webb/Norbert Wolf,* catalogue, Museum Haus Lange, Krefeld, 1980
Hamish Keith, *Boyd Webb: Photographic Works 1976-1981,* catalogue Auckland City Art Gallery, 1981
Michael Schwarz, *Boyd Webb,* catalogue, Badischer Kunstverein, Karlsruhe, 1982
John Roberts, 'A Twist in the Tail: Boyd Webb and the Directorial Tradition', catalogue insert, Badischer Kunstverein, Karlsruhe, 1982
Bernard Blistene, 'Losing Your Bearings', *Boyd Webb,* Stedelijk Van Abbemuseum, Eindhoven, 1983
Gerald van der Kaap, 'Boyd Webb', *Artforum,* November, 1983
Stuart Morgan, 'Boyd Webb', *Beaux Arts Magazine,* No. 13, May, 1984
Ian Walker, 'Boyd Webb', *Creative Camera,* No. 23, December, 1984
Stuart Morgan, 'Boyd Webb Interviewed', *Creative Camera,* No. 23, December, 1984
Stuart Morgan, 'Scenes and Songs from Boyd Webb', *Artforum,* November, 1984
Patrick Kinmonth, 'Neo-Logic of Boyd Webb', *Vogue,* February, 1985
Rommert Boonstra, 'Fotograaf Boyd Webb en de Werkelijkheid van de Schijn', *Avenue,* July, 1985
Kim Levin, 'Boyd Webb', Art Talk, *Village Voice,* 22 October, 1985
Lynne Cooke, 'Boyd Webb', *Nouvelle Biennale de Paris,* catalogue, Electra Moniteur, Paris, 1985
Rolf Paltzer, 'Tauschung um der Wahrheit willen', *Art das Kunstmagazin,* No. 11, November, 1985
Stephen Ellis, 'Boyd Webb at Sonnabend', *Art in America,* January, 1986
Stuart Morgan, 'Paper Moon', *Parkett,* No. 9, 1986
Richard Cork, *Boyd Webb,* catalogue, Adelaide Festival of Arts, 1986
Stuart Morgan, 'Boyd Webb', *Prospect 86,* Frankfurter Kunstverein, 1986
'Inanimations', project for Artforum, April, 1987

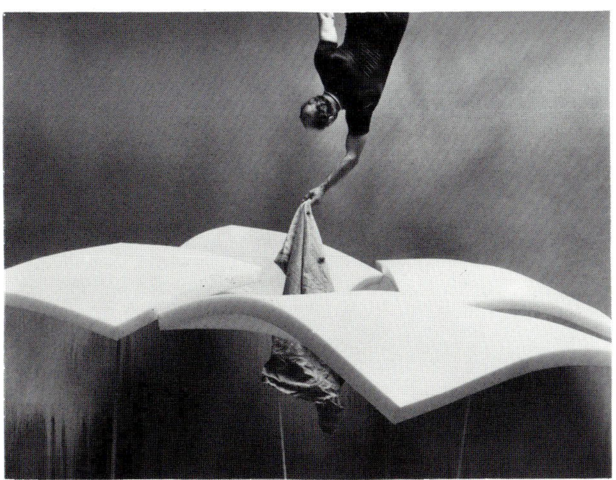

Scott's Tent, 1984,
Unique colour photograph, 122 × 152 cms,
The Trustees of the Tate Gallery, London

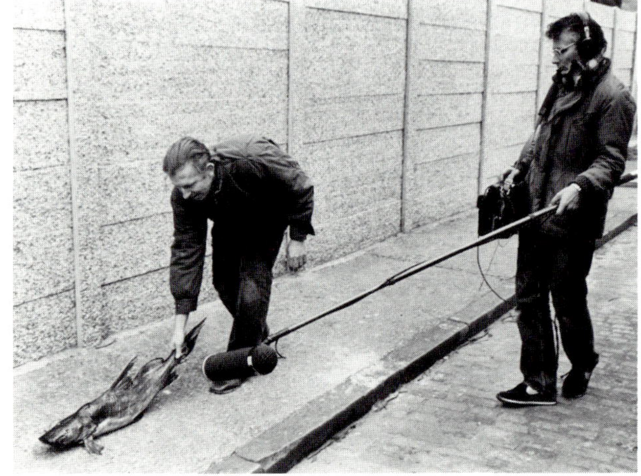

As Yet Undrawn, 1985,
Unique colour photograph, 152 × 120 cms,
Galerie Schurr, Stuttgart

Films

Scenes and Songs from Boyd Webb, 1984, directed by
Philip Haas, colour, 20 minutes, 16 mm, Arts Council of
Great Britain

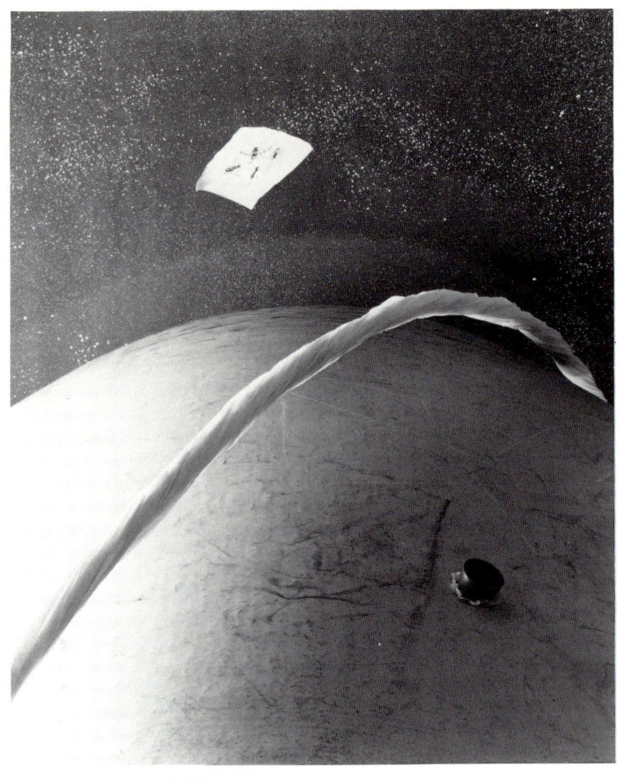

From the film *Scenes and Songs from Boyd Webb*

The Whitechapel Art Gallery opened in 1901 and is administered by a charitable trust. The trust has no endowment and the Gallery's existence and programme therefore depend wholly on financial assistance given by national and local authorities, companies (through sponsorship and donations), foundations, trusts and individuals. In 1984, the Whitechapel Art Gallery Foundation was established to stimulate support from the business community and charitable sector.

The Whitechapel gratefully acknowledges the financial assistance which it has been receiving from:

Arts Council of Great Britain Greater London Arts
London Borough of Tower of Hamlets
London Boroughs Grants Scheme
Inner London Education Authority

Foundations and Trusts
Aldgate and Allhallows, Barking Exhibition Foundation
Clothworkers' Company Drapers' Company
The Henry Moore Foundation Mercers' Company
Ruskin's Guild of St George Sir John Cass's Foundation

Sponsors
Bankers Trust Company Global Asset Management
Marks and Spencer plc Midland Bank

Corporate Patrons
Blackwall Green Ltd Cable and Wireless plc
Citicorp Investment Bank Ltd
City Acre Property Investment Trust
Credit Suisse First Boston Ltd E D & F Man International Ltd
Euromoney Granada Group plc
Henry Ansbacher & Co Ltd Hogg Robinson (Travel) Ltd
Midland Bank More O'Ferrall plc The Morgan Bank
Morgan Stanley International National Westminster Bank plc
Nomura International Finance plc
Officescape Ltd Pearson plc Peat Marwick
Price Waterhouse Romulus Construction Ltd
S J Crowley Ltd Saatchi & Saatchi Company plc
Salomon Brothers International Ltd
Scrimgeour Vickers (Corporate Finance) Ltd Sotheby's
Steggles Palmer Taylor Woodrow Group Trafalgar House plc
Waddington Galleries Ltd Watney, Mann and Truman Ltd
Williams Lea & Co Ltd

Corporate Associates
Alex Reid & Lefevre Ltd Anthony d'Offay Gallery
The Bank of England BET plc Christie, Manson & Woods Ltd
Edward Totah Gallery The Fine Art Society
Fischer Fine Art Ltd Galerie Maeght Lelong, New York
Goldman Sachs International Corp
Juda Rowan Gallery Kleinwort, Benson, Lonsdale plc
Knoedler Kasmin Ltd Lisson Gallery London Ltd
Marlborough Fine Art (London) Ltd Mayor Gallery Ltd
Morgan Grenfell & Co Ltd MoMart Ltd
National Investment Group plc Nicola Jacobs Gallery
Robert Fleming Holdings Ltd
N M Rothschild & Sons Ltd Royal Insurance plc
Sedgwick Group plc Sun Life Assurance Society plc
S G Warburg & Co Ltd Thames and Hudson Ltd
The International Stock Exchange The Rank Organisation plc
Victoria Miro Gallery, London